The Little Book of GREAT LINES FROM SHAKESPEARE

The Little Book of GREAT LINES FROM SHAKESPEARE

Edited by

NICK DE SOMOGYI

SIENA

This edition published and distributed by Siena, 1998

Siena is an imprint of Parragon

Parragon
13 Whiteladies Road
Clifton
Bristol BS8 1PB

Produced by Magpie Books, an imprint of
Robinson Publishing Ltd, London

Cover illustration courtesy of The Bridgeman Art Library

ISBN 0 75252 689 8

A copy of the British Library Cataloguing-in-Publication Data is available from the British Library

Contents

Introduction

There comes a moment in Shakespeare's King Lear when the blind Duke of Gloucester is led to the steep verge of Dover cliff. "How fearful and dizzy 'tis to cast one's eyes so low!" says his companion; "The crows and choughs that wing the midway air | Show scarce so gross as beetles . . . The murmuring surge . . . Cannot be heard so high." A few moments later he jumps off the cliff – yet miraculously survives. "Have I fallen or no?" he asks a third man at the bottom, who replies:

> *From the dread summit of this chalky bourn!*
> *Look up a-height: the shrill-gorged lark so far*
> *Cannot be seen or heard.*

But the man who talks to him at the top of the cliff is the same man who meets him at the bottom – his own son Edgar in another disguise; he has not fallen; and, finally, there is no such cliff.

Open to the elements of daylight sky (where crows and larks perhaps winged the midway air), there were no "special effects" or scenery in the little wooden O of the Globe playhouse, where King Lear *was first performed. Shakespeare's audiences were all like blind Gloucester, led by the suggestive power of his words, and the force of their performance, into believing in something that wasn't there. As he earlier wrote, in a play set on a midsummer's night (but performed during the day):*

> *The poet's eye, in a fine frenzy rolling,*
> *Doth glance from heaven to earth, from earth to heaven,*
> *And as imagination bodies forth*
> *The forms of things unknown, the poet's pen*
> *Turns them to shapes, and gives to airy nothing*
> *A local habitation and a name.*

The effect of Shakespeare's words on our mind's eye (a phrase Shakespeare invented) is as fearful and dizzy as the cliff he conjured out of airy nothing 400 years ago, only to disappear again into thin air (another phrase Shakespeare invented). Here are some of those words.

Chapter 1

WORDS, WORDS, WORDS

Shakespeare was fascinated both by the power and the frailty of language. How is it that "a scribbled form, drawn with a pen" can turn into a tavern-bill or a love-poem? "Words are but wind," yet they can breathe life into rousing oratory or bitter curses. "What's in a name?"

Words, words, words

Prince Hamlet, *Hamlet*

POLONIUS: What do you read, my lord?
HAMLET: Words, words, words.
POLONIUS: What is the matter, my lord?
HAMLET: Between who?
POLONIUS: I mean the matter you read, my lord.
HAMLET: Slanders, sir.

One little word

Bolingbroke, *Richard II*

KING: Uncle, even in the glasses of thine eyes
I see thy grieved heart. Thy sad aspect
Hath from the number of his banished years
Plucked four away. Six frozen winters spent,
Return with welcome home from banishment.
BOLINGBROKE: How long a time lies in one little word!
Four lagging winters and four wanton springs
End in a word: such is the breath of kings.
GAUNT: I thank my liege that in regard of me
He shortens four years of my son's exile.

Honorificabilitudinitatibus

Costard, *Love's Labour's Lost*

ARMADO: Man of peace, well encountered!
HOLOFERNES: Most military sir, salutation!
MOTH: They have been at a great feast of languages and stolen the scraps.
COSTARD: O, they have lived long on the alms-basket of words. I marvel thy master hath not eaten thee for a word, for thou art not so long by the head as "honorificabilitudinitatibus". Thou art easier swallowed than a flap-dragon.

It was Greek to me

Casca, *Julius Caesar*

BRUTUS: And after that he came thus sad away?
CASCA: Ay.
CASSIUS: Did Cicero say anything?
CASCA: Ay, he spoke Greek.
CASSIUS: Nay an I tell you that, I'll ne'er look you i' th' face again. But those that understood him smiled at one another, and shook their heads. But for mine own part, it was Greek to me.

And for my name of George begins with G

Clarence, *Richard III*

RICHARD: But what's the matter, Clarence? May I know?

CLARENCE: Yea, Richard, when I know, for I protest
As yet I know not. But as I can learn,
He hearkens after prophecies and dreams,
And from the cross-row plucks the letter G
And says a wizard told him that by G
His issue disinherited should be.
And for my name of George begins with G
It follows in his thought that I am he!

I had a wound here that was like a T

Scarus, *Antony and Cleopatra*

ANTONY: Thou bleed'st apace.

SCARUS: I had a wound here that was like a T.
But now 'tis made an H.

Thus makes she her great P's

Malvolio, reading a letter, *Twelfth Night*

MALVOLIO: By my life, this is my lady's hand! These be her very C's, her U's and her T's, and thus makes she her great P's. It is, contempt of question, her hand. "To the unknown beloved, this, and my good wishes". Her very phrases! By your leave, wax. Soft! – and the impressure her Lucrece, with which she uses to seal. 'Tis my lady! To whom should this be?

Thou whoreson Z

Kent, *King Lear*

CORNWALL: Speak yet! How grew your quarrel?
OSWALD: This ancient ruffian, sir, whose life I have spared at suit of his grey beard –
KENT: Thou whoreson Z, thou unnecessary letter!

A comma 'tween their amities

Prince Hamlet, *Hamlet*

HAMLET: Wilt thou know
Th' effect of what I wrote?
HORATIO: Ay, good my lord.
HAMLET: An earnest conjuration from the King,
As England was his faithful tributary,
As love between them like the palm should flourish,
As peace should still her wheaten garland wear
And stand a comma 'tween their amities,
And many such like "as"es of great charge,
That on the view and know of these contents
Without debatement further more or less
He should the bearers put to sudden death.

A half-moon, made with a pen

Mamillius, *The Winter's Tale*

FIRST LADY: Shall I be your play-fellow?
MAMILLIUS: No, I'll none of you.
FIRST LADY: Why, my sweet lord?
MAMILLIUS: You'll kiss me hard, and speak to me as if
I were a baby still. I love you better.
SECOND LADY: And why so, my lord?
MAMILLIUS: Not for because
Your brows are blacker (yet black brows, they say,
Become some women best, so that there be not
Too much hair here, but in a semi-circle
Or a half-moon, made with a pen).

Item: two lips

Olivia, *Twelfth Night*

VIOLA [*disguised as Cesario*]:
Lady you are the cruell'st she alive
If you will lead these graces to the grave
And leave the world no copy.

OLIVIA: O sir, I will not be so hard-hearted. I will give out divers schedules of my beauty. It shall be inventoried and every particle and utensil labelled to my will, as "Item: two lips, indifferent red. Item: two grey eyes, with lids to them. Item: one neck, one chin" and so forth. Were you sent hither to praise me?

VIOLA: I see what you are. You are too proud.

Item: sack, two gallons

Falstaff's bill, *Henry IV, Part One*

PETO: Fast alseep behind the arras, and snorting like a horse.
HAL: Hark how hard he fetches breath – search his pockets. What hast thou found?
PETO: Nothing but papers, my lord.
HAL: Let's see what they be, read them.
PETO [*reads*]:

Item: a capon ....*2s. 2d.*
Item: sauce..*4d.*
Item: sack, two gallons...................................*5s. 8d.*
Item: anchovies and sack after supper ....*2s. 6d.*
Item: bread ....*ob.*

HAL: O monstrous! But one halfpennyworth of bread to this intolerable deal of sack!

I will write all down

Iachimo, spying on Imogen, *Cymbeline*

I will write all down.
Such and such pictures, there the window, such
Th' adornment of her bed, the arras, figures,
Why, such and such; and the contents o' th' story.
Ah, but some natural notes about her body
Above ten thousand meaner moveables
Would testify t'enrich mine inventory.
O sleep, thou ape of death, lie dull upon her,
And be her sense but as a monument
Thus in a chapel lying. Come off, come off,
As slippery as the Gordian knot was hard!
'Tis mine – and this will witness outwardly
As strongly as the conscience does within,
To th' madding of her lord. On her left breast
A mole, cinque-spotted, like the crimson drops
I' th' bottom of a cowslip. Here's a voucher
Stronger than ever law could make. This secret
Will force him think I have picked the lock and ta'en
The treasure of her honour.

A book where men may read strange matters

Lady Macbeth, *Macbeth*

Your face, my thane, is as a book where men
May read strange matters. To beguile the time,
Look like the time; bear welcome in your eye,
Your hand, your tongue. Look like the innocent flower,
But be the serpent under't.

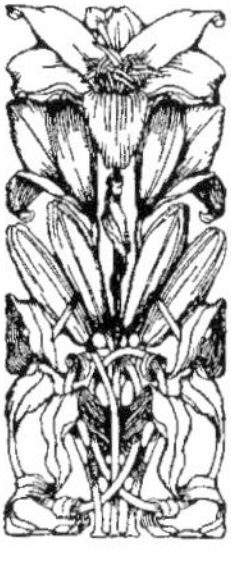

The book and volume of my brain

Prince Hamlet, *Hamlet*

Remember thee?
Ay, thou poor ghost, while memory holds a seat
In this distracted globe. Remember thee?
Yea, from the table of my memory
I'll wipe away all trivial fond records,
All saws of books, all forms, all pressures past,
That youth and observation copied there,
And thy commandment all alone shall live
Within the book and volume of my brain,
Unmixed with baser matter. Yes, by heaven.
O most pernicious woman!
O villain, villain, smiling, damned villain!
My tables, meet it is I set it down
That one may smile and smile and be a villain.
At least I'm sure it may be so in Denmark.

I am for whole volumes in folio!

Armado, *Love's Labour's Lost*

Adieu valour! Rust, rapier! Be still, drum! For your manager is in love; yea, he loveth. Assist me, some extemporal god of rhyme, for I am sure I shall turn sonnet. Devise, wit, write, pen; for I am for whole volumes in folio!

Why is my verse so barren of new pride?

Sonnet 76

Why is my verse so barren of new pride,
So far from variation or quick change?
Why with the time do I not glance aside
To new-found methods, and to compounds strange?
Why write I still all one, ever the same,
And keep invention in a noted weed,
That every word doth almost tell my name,
Showing their birth, and where they did proceed?
O know, sweet love, I always write of you,
And you and love are still my argument.
So all my best is dressing old words new,
Spending again what is already spent:
  For as the sun is daily new and old,
  So is my love still telling what is told.

Truth tired with iteration

Troilus, *Troilus and Cressida*

True swains in love shall in the world to come
Approve their truth by Troilus. When their rhymes,
Full of protest, of oath and big compare,
Wants similes, truth tired with iteration –
"As true as steel, as plantage to the moon,
As sun to day, as turtle to her mate,
As iron to adamant, as earth to th' centre" –
Yet after all comparisons of truth,
As truth's authentic author to be cited,
"As true as Troilus" shall crown up the verse
And sanctify the numbers.

Letters capital

King Edward, *Edward III*

"Her hair, far softer than the silk worms twist;
Like to a flattering glass, doth make more fair
The yellow amber" – "Like a flattering glass"
Comes in too soon. For, writing of her eyes
I'll say that like a glass they catch the sun,
And thence the hot reflection doth rebound
Against my breast and burns my heart within.
Ah what a world of descant makes my soul
Upon this voluntary ground of love!
Come, Lodovic, hast thou turned thy ink to gold?
If not, write but in letters capital
My mistress' name, and it will gild thy paper.
Read, lord, read:
Fill thou the empty hollows of mine ears
With the sweet hearing of thy poetry!

"The most beautified Ophelia"

Polonius, reading Prince Hamlet's letter, *Hamlet*

POLONIUS: I have a daughter – whilst she is mine –
Who in her duty and obedience, mark,
Hath given me this. Now, gather and surmise:
"To the celestial and my soul's idol, the most beautified Ophelia" – that's an ill phrase, a vile phrase, "beautified" is a vile phrase! But you shall hear – "these in her excellent white bosom, these".

Who will believe my verse in time to come?

Sonnet 17

Who will believe my verse in time to come
If it were filled with your most high deserts?
Though yet, heaven knows, it is but as a tomb
Which hides your life, and shows not half your parts.
If I could write the beauty of your eyes
And in fresh numbers number all your graces,
The age to come would say, "This poet lies!
Such heavenly touches ne'er touched earthly faces!"
So should my papers, yellowed with their age,
Be scorned, like old men of less truth than tongue,
And your true rights be termed a poet's rage
And stretched metre of an antique song.
  But were some child of yours alive that time,
  You should live twice: in it and in my rhyme.

Our poesy is as a gum which oozes

Poet, *Timon of Athens*

PAINTER: You are rapt, sir, in some work?
Some dedication to the great lord?
POET: A thing slipped idly from me.
Our poesy is as a gum which oozes
From whence 'tis nourish'd. The fire i' th' flint
Shows not till it be struck. Our gentle flame
Provokes itself, and, like the current, flies
Each bound it chases.

~

Nothing so much as mincing poetry

Hotspur, *Henry IV, Part One*

I had rather be a kitten and cry "mew"
Than one of these same metre-ballad-mongers!
I had rather hear a brazen candlestick turn'd,
Or a dry wheel grate on the axle-tree,
And that would set my teeth nothing on edge,
Nothing so much as mincing poetry!
'Tis like the forced gait of a shuffling nag.

Mere words

Troilus, *Troilus and Cressida*

PANDARUS: What says she there?
TROILUS [*tearing Cressida's letter*]:
Words, words, mere words, no matter from the heart.

~

A deed without a name

The Witches, *Macbeth*

MACBETH: How now, you secret, black, and midnight hags,
What is't you do?
WITCHES: A deed without a name.

What's in a name?

Juliet, *Romeo and Juliet*

'Tis but thy name that is my enemy.
Thou art thyself, though not a Montague.
What's Montague? It is nor hand, nor foot,
Nor arm, nor face, nor any other part
Belonging to a man. O be some other name!
What's in a name? That which we call a rose
By any other word would smell as sweet.

What is honour? A word

Falstaff, *Henry IV, Part One*

Well, 'tis no matter, honour pricks me on. Yea, but how if honour prick me off when I come on? How then? Can honour set a leg? No. Or an arm? No. Or take away the grief of a wound? No. Honour hath no skill in surgery, then? No. What is honour? A word. What is in that word "honour"? Air. A trim reckoning! Who hath it? He that died o' Wednesday. Doth he feel it? No. Doth he hear it? No. 'Tis insensible then? Yea, to the dead. But will it not live with the living? No. Why? Detraction will not suffer it. Therefore, I'll none of it. Honour is mere scutcheon. And so ends my catechism.

Good name in man and woman

Iago, *Othello*

Good name in man and woman, dear my lord,
Is the immediate jewel of their souls.
Who steals my purse steals trash; 'tis something, nothing;
'Twas mine, 'tis his, and has been slave to thousands.
But he that filches from me my good name
Robs me of that which not enriches him
And makes me poor indeed.

There's language in her eye, her cheek, her lip

Ulysses, *Troilus and Cressida*

Fie, fie upon her!
There's language in her eye, her cheek, her lip,
Nay her foot speaks. Her wanton spirits look out
At every joint and motive of her body.
O these encounterers so glib of tongue,
That give accosting welcome ere it comes,
And wide unclasp the tables of their thoughts
To every ticklish reader, set them down
For sluttish spoils of opportunity
And daughters of the game.

You taught me language

Caliban, *The Tempest*

MIRANDA: I pitied thee
Took pains to make thee speak, taught thee each hour
One thing or other. When thou didst not, savage,
Know thine own meaning, but wouldst gabble like
A thing most brutish, I endowed thy purposes
With words that made them known. But thy vile race,
Though thou didst learn, had that in't which good natures
Could not abide to be with; therefore wast thou
Deservedly confined into this rock,
Who hadst deserved more than a prison.
CALIBAN: You taught me language, and my profit on't
Is I know how to curse. The red plague rid you
For learning me your language!

Words are but wind

Dromio of Ephesus, *The Comedy of Errors*

A man may break a word with you, sir, and words are but wind;
Ay, and break it in your face, so he break it not behind.

This day is called the Feast of Crispian . . .

King Henry, *Henry V*

This day is called the Feast of Crispian.
He that outlives this day and comes safe home
Will stand a-tiptoe when this day is named.
And rouse him at the name of Crispian.
He that shall see this day and live t'old age
Will yearly on the vigil feast his neighbours
And say, "Tomorrow is Saint Crispian."
Then will he strip his sleeve and show his scars,
And say, "These wounds I had on Crispin's day."
Old men forget; yet all shall be forgot,
But he'll remember, with advantages,
What feats he did that day.

. . . We few, we happy few

King Henry, *Henry V*

Then shall our names,
Familiar in his mouth as household words -
Harry the King, Bedford, and Exeter,
Warwick and Talbot, Salisbury and Gloucester –
Be in their flowing cups freshly remembered.
This story shall the good man teach his son,
And Crispin Crispian shall ne'er go by
From this day to the ending of the world
But we in it shall be remembered,
We few, we happy few, we band of brothers.
For he today that sheds his blood with me
Shall be my brother; be he ne'er so vile,
This day shall gentle his condition.
And gentlemen in England now abed
Shall think themselves accursed they were not here
And hold their manhoods cheap whiles any speaks
That fought with us upon Saint Crispin's day.

But will they come?

Hotspur, *Henry IV, Part One*

MORTIMER: Peace, cousin Percy, you will make him mad.
GLENDOWER: I can call spirits from the vasty deep!
HOTSPUR: Why, so can I, or so can any man.
But will they come when you do call for them?

Friends, Romans, countrymen

Mark Antony, *Julius Caesar*

Friends, Romans, countrymen, lend me your ears.
I come to bury Caesar, not to praise him.
The evil that men do lives after them;
The good is oft interred with their bones.
So let it be with Caesar. The noble Brutus
Hath told you Caesar was ambitious.
If it were so, it was a grievous fault,
And grievously hath Caesar answered it.
Here, under leave of Brutus and the rest
(For Brutus is an honourable man,
So are they all, all honourable men),
Come I to speak in Caesar's funeral.
He was my friend, faithful and just to me,
But Brutus says he was ambitious,
And Brutus is an honourable man.

My words fly up, my thoughts remain below

Claudius, *Hamlet*

My words fly up, my thoughts remain below.
Words without thoughts never to heaven go.

By heaven, he echoes me

Othello, *Othello*

IAGO: I did not think he had been acquainted with her.
OTHELLO: Oh yes, and went between us very often.
IAGO: Indeed?
OTHELLO: "Indeed"? Indeed. Discern'st thou aught in that?
Is he not honest?
IAGO: Honest, my lord?
OTHELLO: "Honest"? Ay, honest.
IAGO: My lord, for aught I know.
OTHELLO: What dost thou think?
IAGO: Think, my lord?
OTHELLO: "Think, my lord"? By heaven, he echoes me,
As if there were monster in his thought,
Too hideous to be shown.

Upon my tongues continual slanders ride

Rumour the Prologue, *Henry IV, Part Two*

Upon my tongues continual slanders ride,
The which in every language I pronounce,
Stuffing the ears of men with false reports.
I speak of peace, while covert enmity
Under the smile of safety wounds the world.
And who but Rumour, who but only I,
Make fearful musters and prepared defence
Whiles the big year, swoll'n with some other grief,
Is thought with child by the stern tyrant war,
And no such matter? Rumour is a pipe
Blown by surmises, jealousies, conjectures,
And of so easy and so plain a stop
That the blunt monster with uncounted heads,
The still-discordant wav'ring multitude,
Can play upon it.

Is not the truth the truth?

Falstaff, *Henry IV, Part One*

FALSTAFF: But as the devil would have it, three misbegotten knaves in Kendal green came at my back and let drive at me, for it was so dark, Hal, that thou couldst not see thy hand.
HAL: These lies are like their father that begets them – gross as a mountain, open, palpable. Why thou clay-brained guts, thou knotty-pated fool, thou whoreson obscene greasy tallow-catch –
FALSTAFF: What, art thou mad? Art thou mad? Is not the truth the truth?
HAL: Why, how couldst thou know these men in Kendal green when it was so dark thou couldst not see thy hand?

Is there no offence in't?

Claudius, *Hamlet*

HAMLET: Madam, how like you this play?
GERTRUDE: The lady protests too much, methinks.
HAMLET: Oh but she'll keep her word.
CLAUDIUS: Have you heard the argument? Is there no offence in't?
HAMLET: No, no, they do but jest, poison in jest. No offence i' th' world.

Art made tongue-tied by authority

Sonnet 66

And art made tongue-tied by authority,
And folly, doctor-like, controlling skill,
And simple truth miscalled simplicity,
And captive good attending captain ill.

To define true madness

Polonius, *Hamlet*

Therefore, since brevity is the soul of wit,
And tediousness the limbs and outward flourishes,
I will be brief. Your noble son is mad –
Mad call I it, for to define true madness.
What is't but to be nothing else but mad?
But let that go.

A document in madness!

Laertes, *Hamlet*

OPHELIA: There's rosemary, that's for remembrance. Pray, love, remember. And there is pansies; that's for thoughts.
LAERTES: A document in madness! Thoughts and remembrance fitted.

The written troubles of the brains

Macbeth, *Macbeth*

MACBETH: How does your patient, doctor?
DOCTOR: Not so sick, my lord,
As she is troubled with thick-coming fancies
That keep her from her rest.
MACBETH: Cure her of that.
Canst thou not minister to a mind diseased,
Pluck from the memory a rooted sorrow?
Raze out the written troubles of the brain,
And with some sweet oblivious antidote
Cleanse the fraught bosom of that perilous stuff
Which weighs upon the heart?

Life is as tedious as a twice-told tale

The Dauphin, *King John*

There's nothing in this world can make me joy.
Life is as tedious as a twice-told tale,
Vexing the dull ear of a drowsy man;
And bitter shame hath spoiled the sweet world's taste,
That it yields naught but shame and bitterness.

If it be nothing, I shall not need spectacles

Gloucester, *King Lear*

GLOUCESTER: What paper were you reading?
EDMUND: Nothing, my lord.
GLOUCESTER: No? What needed then that terrible dispatch of it into your pocket? The quality of nothing hath not need to hide itself. Let's see. Come, if it be nothing, I shall not need spectacles.

Nothing will come of nothing

Lear, *King Lear*

LEAR: What can you say to draw
A third more opulent than your sisters? Speak.
CORDELIA: Nothing.
LEAR: Nothing?
CORDELIA: Nothing.
LEAR: Nothing will come of nothing. Speak again.
CORDELIA: Unhappy that I am, I cannot heave
My heart into my mouth. I love your majesty
According to my bond, no more nor less.

A pound of flesh

Portia, *The Merchant of Venice*

SHYLOCK: I pray thee, pursue sentence.
PORTIA: A pound of that same merchant's flesh is thine.
The court awards it, and the law doth give it.
SHYLOCK: Most rightful judge!
PORTIA: And you must cut this flesh from off his breast.
The law allows it, and the court awards it.
SHYLOCK: Most learned judge! A sentence! Come, prepare.
PORTIA: Tarry a little. There is something else.
This bond doth give thee here no jot of blood.
The words expressly are "a pound of flesh".
Take then thy bond. Take thou thy pound of flesh.
But in the cutting it, if thou dost shed
One drop of Christian blood, thy lands and goods
Are (by the laws of Venice) confiscate
Unto the state of Venice.

Neither a borrower nor a lender be

Polonius, *Hamlet*

Beware
Of entrance to a quarrel, but being in,
Bear't that th'opposed may beware of thee.
Give every man thine ear but few thy voice.
Take each man's censure, but reserve thy judgement.
Costly thy habit as thy purse can buy,
But not expressed in fancy; rich not gaudy;
For the apparel oft proclaims the man,
And they in France of the best rank and station
Are of all most select and generous chief in that.
Neither a borrower nor a lender be,
For loan oft loses both itself and friend,
And borrowing dulls the edge of husbandry.
This above all: to thine own self be true.
And it must follow, as the night the day,
Thou canst not then be false to any man.

Let's kill all the lawyers!

The Butcher, *Henry VI, Part Two*

CADE: And when I am king, as king I will be –
REBELS: God save your majesty!
CADE: I thank you, good people! – there shall be no money. All shall eat and drink on my score, and I will apparel them all in one livery that they may agree like brothers, and worship me their lord.
BUTCHER: The first thing we do, let's kill all the lawyers!
CADE: Nay that I mean to do. Is not this a lamentable thing that of a skin of an innocent lamb should be made parchment? That parchment, being scribbled o'er, should undo a man?

A scribbled form, drawn with a pen

John, *King John*

Ay marry, now my soul hath elbow-room.
It would not out at windows nor at doors.
There is so hot a summer in my bosom
That all my bowels crumble up to dust.
I am a scribbled form, drawn with a pen
Upon a parchment, and against this fire
Do I shrink up.

Let's choose executors and talk of wills

King Richard, *Richard II*

Let's talk of graves, of worms and epitaphs,
Make dust our paper, and with rainy eyes,
Write sorrow on the bosom of the earth.
Let's choose executors and talk of wills –
And yet not so, for what can we bequeath
Save our deposed bodies to the ground?

The words of Mercury are harsh after the songs of Apollo

Armado, *Love's Labour's Lost*

The words of Mercury are harsh after the songs of Apollo. You that way; we this way.
Exeunt, severally

Chapter 2

THE GREAT GLOBE ITSELF

"This is Illyria, lady" (Twelfth Night); *"Denmark's a prison"* (Hamlet). *Shakespeare's plays transport us, in our mind's eye, across the world of space and time to the merchant's Venice, the two gentlemen's Verona, and the "brave new world" of* The Tempest. *The playhouse in which he acted was named after the world, but as his famous lines from* As You Like It *tell us, the world is also a stage . . .*

All the world's a stage . . .

Jaques, *As You Like It*

All the world's a stage,
And all the men and women merely players.
They have their exits and their entrances,
And one man in his time plays many parts,
His acts being seven ages. At first the infant,
Mewling and puking in the nurse's arms.
Then, the whining schoolboy with his satchel
And shining morning face, creeping like snail
Unwillingly to school. And then the lover,
Sighing like furnace, with a woeful ballad
Made to his mistress' eyebrow. Then a soldier,
Full of strange oaths, and bearded like the pard,
Jealous in honour, sudden, and quick in quarrel,
Seeking the bubble reputation
Even in the cannon's mouth.

. . . Last scene of all

Jaques, *As You Like It*

And then the justice,
In fair round belly, with good capon lined
With eyes severe, and beard of formal cut,
Full of wise saws, and modern instances,
And so he plays his part. The sixth age shifts
Into the lean and slippered pantaloon,
With spectacles on nose and pouch on side,
His youthful hose well saved, a world too wide
For his shrunk shank, and his big manly voice
Turning again toward childish treble, pipes
And whistles in his sound. Last scene of all,
That ends this strange eventful history,
Is second childishness and mere oblivion,
Sans teeth, sans eye, sans taste, sans everything.

I know not "seems"

Prince Hamlet, *Hamlet*

GERTRUDE: Thou know'st 'tis common: all that lives must die,
Passing through nature to eternity.
HAMLET: Ay, madam, 'tis common.
GERTRUDE: If it be,
Why seems it so particular with thee?
HAMLET: "Seems", madam? Nay, it is. I know not "seems".
'Tis not alone my inky cloak, good mother,
Nor customary suits of solemn black,
Nor windy suspirations of forced breath,
No, nor the fruitful river in the eye,
Nor the dejected 'haviour of the visage,
Together with all forms, moods, shows of grief
That can denote me truly. These indeed "seem",
For they are actions that a man might play.
But I have that within which passeth show,
These but the trappings and the suits of woe.

This green plot shall be our stage

Quince, *A Midsummer Night's Dream*

Here's a marvellous convenient place for our rehearsal. This green plot shall be our stage; this hawthorn-brake our tiring-house; and we will do it in action, as we will do it before the Duke.

Tragical-comical-historical-pastoral

Polonius, *Hamlet*

The best actors in the world, either for tragedy, comedy, history, pastoral, pastoral-comical, historical-pastoral, tragical-historical, tragical-comical-historical-pastoral, scene individable, or poem unlimited.

In King Cambyses' vein

Falstaff, *Henry IV, Part One*

PRINCE HAL: Do thou stand for my father and examine me upon the particulars of my life.

FALSTAFF: Shall I? Content! This chair shall be my state, this dagger my sceptre, and this cushion my crown.

PRINCE HAL: Thy state is taken for a joint-stool, thy golden sceptre for a leaden dagger, and thy precious rich crown for a pitiful bald crown.

FALSTAFF: Well, and the fire of grace be not quite out of thee, now shalt thou be moved. Give me a cup of sack to make my eyes look red, that it may be thought I have wept, for I must speak in passion, and I will do it in King Cambyses' vein.

Thrice-gorgeous Ceremony

King Henry, *Henry V*

'Tis not the balm, the sceptre, and the ball,
The sword, the mace, the crown imperial,
The intertissued robe of gold and pearl,
The farced title running 'fore the king,
The throne he sits on nor the tide of pomp
That beats upon the high shore of this world –
No, not all these, thrice-gorgeous Ceremony,
Not all these, laid in bed majestical,
Can sleep so soundly as the wretched slave
Who with a body filled and vacant mind
Gets him to rest, crammed with distressed bread.

Tomorrow, and tomorrow, and tomorrow

Macbeth, *Macbeth*

SEYTON: The Queen, my lord, is dead.
MACBETH: She should have died hereafter:
There would have been a time for such a word.
Tomorrow, and tomorrow, and tomorrow,
Creeps in this petty pace from day to day,
To the last syllable of recorded time;
And all our yesterdays have lighted fools
The way to dusty death. Out, out, brief candle!
Life's but a walking shadow; a poor player,
That struts and frets his hour upon the stage,
And then is heard no more: it is a tale
Told by an idiot, full of sound and fury,
Signifying nothing.

What, household stuff?

Christopher Sly, *The Taming of the Shrew*

PAGE: Your honour's players, hearing your
 amendment,
Are come to play a pleasant comedy.
For so your doctors hold it very meet,
Seeing too much sadness hath congealed your blood,
And melancholy is the nurse of frenzy.
Therefore they thought it good you hear a play
And frame your mind to mirth and merriment,
Which bars a thousand harms and lengthens life.
SLY: Marry, I will. Let them play it. Is not a comedy,
A Christmas gambol or a tumbling-trick?
PAGE: No, my good lord, it is more pleasing stuff.
SLY: What, household stuff?
PAGE: It is a kind of history.

Caviar to the general

Prince Hamlet, *Hamlet*

HAMLET: Come, a passionate speech.
FIRST PLAYER: What speech, my lord?
HAMLET: I heard thee speak me a speech once, but it was never acted, or, if it was, not above once; for the play, I remember, pleased not the million. 'Twas caviar to the general. But it was (as I received it, and others whose judgements in such matters cried in the top of mine) an excellent play, well digested in the scenes, set down with as much modesty as cunning.

This brave o'erhanging firmament

Prince Hamlet, *Hamlet*

I have of late, but wherefore I know not, lost all my mirth, foregone all custom of exercises; and indeed it goes so heavily with my disposition that this goodly frame the earth seems to me a sterile promontory, this most excellent canopy the air, look you, this brave o'erhanging firmament, this majestical roof fretted with golden fire, why, it appeareth nothing to me but a foul and pestilent congregation of vapours.

Such a deal of stinking breath

Casca, *Julius Caesar*

And still as he refused it, the rabblement hooted, and clapped their chapped hands, and threw up their sweaty nightcaps, and uttered such a deal of stinking breath because Caesar refused the crown that it had almost choked Caesar, for he swooned and fell down at it.

~

The fault, dear Brutus, is not in our stars but in ourselves

Cassius, *Julius Caesar*

BRUTUS: I do believe that these applauses are
For some new honours that are heaped on Caesar.
CASSIUS: Why, man, he doth bestride this narrow world
Like a Colossus, and we petty men
Walk under his huge legs, and peep about
To find ourselves dishonourable graves.
Men at some time were masters of their fates.
The fault, dear Brutus, is not in our stars,
But in ourselves that we are underlings.

When I consider everything that grows

Sonnet 15

When I consider everything that grows
Holds in perfection but a little moment;
That this huge stage presenteth naught but shows
Whereon the stars in secret influence comment.
When I perceive that men as plants increase,
Cheered and checked even by the selfsame sky,
Vaunt in their youthful sap, at height decrease,
And wear their brave state out of memory:
Then the conceit of this inconstant stay
Sets you most rich in youth before my sight,
Where wasteful time debateth with decay
To change your day of youth to sullied night.
  And all in war with time for love of you,
  As he takes from you, I engraft you new.

This great stage of fools

Lear, *King Lear*

LEAR: Thou must be patient; we came crying hither:
Thou know'st the first time that we smell the air
We wail and cry. I will preach to thee: mark:
GLOUCESTER: Alack, alack the day!
LEAR: When we are born, we cry that we are come
To this great stage of fools.

Counterfeiting actors

Warwick, *Henry VI, Part Three*

Why stand we like soft-hearted women here,
Wailing our losses, whiles the foe doth rage;
And look upon, as if the tragedy
Were played in jest by counterfeiting actors?

Why, I can smile, and murder whiles I smile

Richard of Gloucester, *Henry VI, Part Three*

Why, I can smile, and murder whiles I smile,
And cry "Content!" to that that grieves my heart,
And wet my cheeks with artificial tears,
And frame my face to all occasions.
I'll drown more sailors than the mermaid shall,
I'll slay more gazers than the basilisk,
I'll play the orator as well as Nestor,
Deceive more slily than Ulysses could,
And like a Sinon take another Troy.
I can add colours to the chameleon,
Change shapes with Proteus for advantages,
And set the murderous Machiavel to school.
Can I do this, and cannot get a crown?
Tut! Were it further off, I'll pluck it down

An improbable fiction

Fabian, *Twelfth Night*

FABIAN: If this were played upon a stage now, I could condemn it as an improbable fiction.

O for a muse of fire

The Chorus, *Henry V*

O for a muse of fire, that would ascend
The brightest heaven of invention,
A kingdom for a stage, princes to act,
And monarchs to behold the swelling scene!
Then should the warlike Harry, like himself,
Assume the port of Mars, and at his heels,
Leashed in like hounds, should famine, sword and fire
Crouch for employment. But pardon, gentles all,
The flat unraised spirits that hath dared
On this unworthy scaffold to bring forth
So great an object. Can this cockpit hold
The vasty fields of France? Or may we cram
Within this wooden O the very casques
That did affright the air at Agincourt?

Industrious scenes and acts of death

The Bastard, *King John*

By Heaven, these scroyles of Angiers flout you, kings,
And stand securely on their battlements,
As in a theatre, whence they gape and point
At your industrious scenes and acts of death.

~

Like a dull actor now I have forgot my part

Caius Martius, *Coriolanus*

Like a dull actor now
I have forgot my part and I am out,
Even to a full disgrace.

Thus play I in one person many people

King Richard, *Richard II*

Thus play I in one person many people,
And none contented. Sometimes am I king,
Then treasons make me wish myself a beggar,
And so I am. Then crushing penury
Persuades me I was better when a king;
Then am I kinged again, and by and by
Think that I am unkinged by Bolingbroke,
And straight am nothing.

Their loud applause and Aves vehement

Duke, *Measure for Measure*

I'll privily away. I love the people,
But do not like to stage me to their eyes.
Though it do well, I do not relish well
Their loud applause and Aves vehement;
Nor do I think the man of safe discretion
That does affect it.

Speak the speech, I pray you . . .

Prince Hamlet, *Hamlet*

Speak the speech, I pray you, as I pronounced it to you, trippingly on the tongue; but if you mouth it as many of your players do, I had as lief the town-crier spoke my lines. Nor do not saw the air too much with your hand, thus, but use all gently; for in the very torrent, tempest, and, as I may say, whirlwind of your passion, you must acquire and beget a temperance that may give it smoothness. Oh it offends me to the soul to hear a robustious periwig-pated fellow tear a passion to tatters, to very rags, to split the ears of the groundlings, who for the most part are capable of nothing but inexplicable dumb-shows and noise. I would have such a fellow whipped for o'erdoing Termagant. It out-herods Herod. Pray you avoid it.

This comedy of Pyramus and Thisbe

Bottom, *A Midsummer Night's Dream*

BOTTOM: Peter Quince!
QUINCE: What sayest thou, bully Bottom?
BOTTOM: There are things in this comedy of Pyramus and Thisbe that will never please. First, Pyramus must draw a sword to kill himself; which the ladies cannot abide. How answer you that?
SNOUT: By'r larkin, a parlous fear!
STARVELING: I believe we must leave the killing out, when all is done.
BOTTOM: Not a whit! I have a device to make all well. Write me a prologue, and let the prologue seem to say we will do no harm with our swords, and that Pyramus is not killed indeed; and for the better assurance, tell them that I, Pyramus, am not Pyramus, but Bottom the weaver. This will put them out of fear.

As happy prologues to the swelling act

Macbeth, *Macbeth*

Two truths are told
As happy prologues to the swelling act
Of the imperial theme.
This supernatural soliciting
Cannot be ill, cannot be good. If ill,
Why hath it given me earnest of success
Commencing in a truth? I am Thane of Cawdor.
If good, why do I yield to that suggestion
Whose horrid image doth unfix my hair
And make my seated heart knock at my ribs
Against the use of nature? Present fears
Are less than horrible imaginings.
My thought, whose murder yet is but fantastical,
Shakes so my single state of man that function
Is smothered in surmise, and nothing is
But what is not.

Ere I could make a prologue to my brains

Prince Hamlet, *Hamlet*

Being thus benetted round with villainies,
Ere I could make a prologue to my brains,
They had begun the play.

He pageants us

Ulysses, *Troilus and Cressida*

He pageants us. Sometime, great Agamemnon,
Thy topless deputation he puts on,
And like a strutting player, whose conceit
Lies in his hamstring and doth think it rich
To hear the wooden dialogue and sound
'Twixt his stretched footing and the scaffoldage,
Such to-be-pitied and o'er-wrested seeming
He acts thy greatness in; and when he speaks,
'Tis like a chime-a-mending, with terms unsquared
Which, from the tongue of roaring Typhon dropped,
Would seem hyperboles. At this fusty stuff
The large Achilles, on his pressed bed lolling,
From his deep chest laughs out a loud applause:
Cries "Excellent! 'Tis Agamemnon right!"

Alas, 'tis true, I have gone here and there

Sonnet 110

Alas, 'tis true, I have gone here and there,
And made myself a motley to the view,
Gored mine own thoughts, sold cheap what is most dear,
Made old offences of affections new.

As an unperfect actor on the stage

Sonnet 23

As an unperfect actor on the stage,
Who with his fear is put besides his part,
Or some fierce thing replete with too much rage,
Whose strength's abundance weakens his own heart;
So I, for fear of trust, forget to say
The perfect ceremony of love's rite,
And in mine own love's strength seem to decay,
O'ercharged with burden of mine own love's might.
O let my books be then the eloquence
And dumb presagers of my speaking breast,
Who plead for love, and look for recompense
More than that tongue that more hath more expressed.
  O learn to read what silent love hath writ;
  To hear with eyes belongs to love's fine wit.

After a well-graced actor leaves the stage

York, *Richard II*

As in a theatre the eyes of men,
After a well-graced actor leaves the stage,
Are idly bent on him that enters next,
Thinking his prattle to be tedious;
Even so, or with much more contempt, men's eyes
Did scowl on Richard. No man cried "God save him!"
No joyful tongue gave him his welcome home,
But dust was thrown upon his sacred head;
Which with such gentle sorrow he shook off,
His face still combating with tears and smiles,
The badges of his grief and patience.

Tut, I can counterfeit the deep tragedian

Buckingham, *Richard III*

RICHARD: Come, cousin, canst thou quake and change thy colour,
Murder thy breath in middle of a word,
And then again begin, and stop again,
As if thou were distraught and mad with terror?
BUCKINGHAM: Tut, I can counterfeit the deep tragedian,
Speak, and look back, and pry on every side,
Tremble and start at wagging of a straw,
Intending deep suspicion. Ghastly looks
Are at my service like enforced smiles,
And both are ready in their offices
At any time to grace my stratagems.

O brave new world!

Miranda, *The Tempest*

How many goodly creatures are there here!
How beauteous mankind is! O brave new world
That has such people in't!

The little O, the earth

Cleopatra, *Antony and Cleopatra*

CLEOPATRA: His face was as the heavens, and therein
  stuck
A sun and moon, which kept their course, and lighted
The little O, the earth.
DOLABELLA: Most sovereign creature –
CLEOPATRA: His legs bestrid the ocean, his reared arm
Crested the world. His voice was propertied
As all the tuned spheres, and that to friends:
But when he meant to quail, and shake the orb,
He was as rattling thunder. For his bounty,
There was no winter in't; an autumn 'twas
That grew the more by reaping: his delights
Were dolphin-like, they showed his back above
The element they lived in. In his livery
Walked crowns and crownets. Realms and islands were
As plates dropped from his pocket.

That's too long for a play

Berowne, *Love's Labour's Lost*

BEROWNE: Our wooing doth not end like an old play:
Jack hath not Jill. These ladies' courtesy
Might well have made our sport a comedy.
KING: Come, sir, it wants a twelvemonth and a day,
And then 'twill end.
BEROWNE: That's too long for a play.

The king's a beggar now the play is done

Epilogue by the King of France,
All's Well That Ends Well

The King's a beggar now the play is done.
All is well ended if this suit be won,
That you express content; which we will pay
With strife to please you, day exceeding day.
Ours be your patience then and yours our parts;
Your gentle hands lend us and take our hearts.

What's Hecuba to him, or he to Hecuba?

Prince Hamlet, *Hamlet*

O what a rogue and peasant slave am I!
Is it not monstrous that this player here,
But in a fiction, in a dream of passion,
Could force his soul so to his own conceit
That from her working all his visage wanned,
Tears in his eyes, distraction in his aspect,
A broken voice, and his whole function suiting
With forms to his conceit? And all for nothing!
For Hecuba!
What's Hecuba to him, or he to Hecuba,
That he should weep for her? What would he do
Had he the motive and the cue for passion
That I have? He would drown the stage with tears,
And cleave the general ear with horrid speech,
Make mad the guilty and appal the free,
Confound the ignorant, and amaze indeed
The very faculties of eyes and ears.

The play's the thing

Prince Hamlet, *Hamlet*

I have heard that guilty creatures sitting at a play
Have, by the very cunning of the scene,
Been struck so to the soul that presently
They have proclaimed their malefactions.
For murder, though it have no tongue, will speak
With most miraculous organ. I'll have these players
Play something like the murder of my father
Before mine uncle. I'll observe his looks;
I'll tent him to the quick. If he do blench,
I know my course. The spirit that I have seen
May be a devil, and the devil hath power
T'assume a pleasing shape, yea, and perhaps
Out of my weakness and my melancholy
As he is very potent with such spirits
Abuses me to damn me. I'll have the grounds
More relative than this. The play's the thing
Wherein I'll catch the conscience of the King.

The two-hours' traffic of our stage

The Chorus, *Romeo and Juliet*

Two households, both alike in dignity
In fair Verona, where we lay our scene,
From ancient grudge break to new mutiny,
Where civil blood makes civil hands unclean.
From forth the fatal loins of these two foes
A pair of star-crossed lovers take their life,
Whose misadventured piteous overthrows
Doth with their death bury their parents' strife.
The fearful passage of their death-marked love
And the continuance of their parents' rage –
Which but their children's end, naught could remove –
Is now the two-hours' traffic of our stage;
  The which if you with patient ears attend,
  What here shall miss, our toil shall strive to mend.

This lofty scene

Cassius, *Julius Caesar*

How many ages hence
Shall this our lofty scene be acted over,
In states unborn, and accents yet unknown!

I did enact Julius Caesar

Polonius, *Hamlet*

HAMLET: My lord, you played once i' th' university, you say?
POLONIUS: That did I, my lord, and was accounted a good actor.
HAMLET: What did you enact?
polonius: I did enact Julius Caesar. I was killed i' th' Capitol. Brutus killed me.
HAMLET: It was a brute part of him to kill so capital a calf there.

Some squeaking Cleopatra boy my greatness

Cleopatra, *Antony and Cleopatra*

CLEOPATRA: Now Iras, what think'st thou?
Thou, an Egyptian puppet shall be shown
In Rome as well as I: mechanic slaves
With greasy aprons, rules, and hammers shall
Uplift us to the view. In their thick breaths
Rank of gross diet, shall we be enclouded,
And forced to drink their vapour.
IRAS: The gods forbid!
CLEOPATRA: Nay, 'tis most certain, Iras: saucy lictors
Will catch at us like strumpets, and scald rhymers
Ballad us out o' tune. The quick comedians
Extemporally will stage us, and present
Our Alexandrian revels. Antony
Shall be brought drunken forth, and I shall see
Some squeaking Cleopatra boy my greatness
I' th' posture of a whore.

The abstract and brief chronicles of the time

Prince Hamlet, *Hamlet*

Good my lord, will you see the players well bestowed? Do you hear? Let them be well used, for they are the abstract and brief chronicles of the time. After your death you were better have a bad epitaph than their ill report while you live.

The better part of valour is discretion

Falstaff, *Henry IV, Part One*

S'blood! 'Twas time to counterfeit, or that hot termagant Scot had paid me, scot and lot too. Counterfeit? I lie, I am no counterfeit. To die is to be a counterfeit, for he is but the counterfeit of a man who hath not the life of a man. But to counterfeit dying when a man thereby liveth is to be no counterfeit, but the true and perfect image of life indeed. The better part of valour is discretion, in the which better part I have saved my life.

Is this a dagger which I see before me?

Macbeth, *Macbeth*

Is this a dagger which I see before me,
The handle toward my hand? Come let me clutch thee.
I have thee not, and yet I see thee still.
Art thou not, fatal vision, sensible
To feeling as to sight? Or art thou but
A dagger of the mind, a false creation
Proceeding from the heat-oppressed brain?

We are such stuff as dreams are made on

Prospero, *The Tempest*

Our revels now are ended. These our actors,
As I foretold you, were all spirits, and
Are melted into air, into thin air:
And, like the baseless fabric of this vision,
The cloud-capped towers, the gorgeous palaces,
The solemn temples, the great globe itself,
Yea all which it inherit, shall dissolve,
And, like this insubstantial pageant faded,
Leave not a rack behind. We are such stuff
As dreams are made on; and our little life
Is rounded with a sleep.

Alas, poor Yorick!

Prince Hamlet, *Hamlet*

GRAVEDIGGER: This same skull, sir, was Yorick's skull, the King's jester.
HAMLET: This?
GRAVEDIGGER: E'en that.
HAMLET: Alas, poor Yorick! I knew him, Horatio, a fellow of infinite jest, of most excellent fancy. He hath bore me on his back a thousand times, and now, how abhorred in my imagination it is. My gorge rises at it. Here hung those lips that I have kissed I know not how oft. Where be your gibes now, your gambols, your songs, your flashes of merriment, that were wont to set the table on a roar? Not one now to mock your own grinning? Quite chop-fallen? Now get you to my lady's chamber and tell her, let her paint an inch thick, to this favour must she come.

Chapter 3

THE MARRIAGE OF TRUE MINDS

The lover, "sighing like a furnace," is the third of Jaques' seven ages of man, but Shakespeare never outgrew his fascination with the comedy and tragedy of love – perhaps because the lover and the poet both give "to airy nothing | A local habitation and a name." From youth to middle age, between love at first sight and the marriage of true minds, for Romeo and Cleopátra, "the course of true love never did run smooth." But what is love?

What is love?

Feste's Song, *Twelfth Night*

What is love? 'Tis not hereafter,
Present mirth hath present laughter.
  What's to come is still unsure.
In delay there lies no plenty,
Then come kiss me, sweet and twenty.
  Youth's a stuff will not endure.

But soft! what light through yonder window breaks?

Romeo, *Romeo and Juliet*

But soft! what light through yonder window breaks?
It is the east, and Juliet is the sun.
Arise, fair sun, and kill the envious moon,
Who is already sick and pale with grief
That thou, fair maid, art far more fair than she.

O Romeo, Romeo, wherefore art thou Romeo?

Juliet, *Romeo and Juliet*

O Romeo, Romeo, wherefore art thou Romeo?
Deny thy father and refuse thy name,
Or if thou willt not, be but sworn my love,
And I'll no longer be a Capulet.

The lunatic, the lover, and the poet

Theseus, *A Midsummer Night's Dream*

Lovers and madmen have such seething brains,
Such shaping fantasies, that apprehend
More than cool reason ever comprehends.
The lunatic, the lover, and the poet
Are of imagination all compact.
One sees more devils than vast hell can hold:
That is the madman. The lover, all as frantic,
Sees Helen's beauty in a brow of Egypt.
The poet's eye, in a fine frenzy rolling,
Doth glance from heaven to earth, from earth to
heaven,
And as imagination bodies forth
The forms of things unknown, the poet's pen
Turns them to shapes, and gives to airy nothing
A local habitation and a name.

See where she comes, apparelled like the spring

Pericles, *Pericles, Prince of Tyre*

See where she comes, apparelled like the spring,
Graces her subjects, and her thoughts the king
Of ev'ry virtue gives renown to men;
Her face the book of praises where is read
Nothing but curious pleasures, as from thence
Sorrow were ever razed, and testy wrath
Could never be her mild companion.
You gods that made me man, and sway in love,
That have inflamed desire in my breast
To taste the fruit of yon celestial tree
Or die in the adventure, be my helps,
As I am son and servant to your will,
To compass such a boundless happiness.

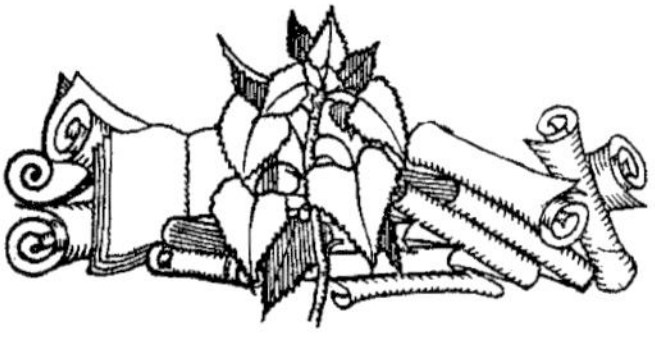

Being your slave, what should I do?

Sonnet 57

Being your slave, what should I do but tend
Upon the hours and times of your desire?
I have no precious time at all to spend,
Nor services to do, till you require.
Nor dare I chide the world-without-end hour
Whilst I, my sovereign, watch the clock for you,
Nor think the bitterness of absence sour,
When you have bid your servant once adieu.
Nor dare I question with my jealous thought
Where you may be, or your affairs suppose,
But like a sad slave stay and think of nought,
Save, where you are, how happy you make those.
So true a fool is love, that in your will,
Though you do anything, he thinks no ill.

Why, how do you know that I am in love?

Valentine, *The Two Gentlemen of Verona*

VALENTINE: Why, how do you know that I am in love?
SPEED: Marry by these special marks: First, you have learned to wreathe your arms, like a malcontent; to relish a love-song, like a robin redbreast; to walk alone, like one that had the pestilence; to sigh, like a schoolboy that had lost his ABC; to weep, like a young wench that had buried her grandam; to fast, like one that takes diet; to watch, like one that fears robbing; to speak puling, like a beggar at Hallowmas.

How silver-sweet sound lovers' tongues by night

Romeo, *Romeo and Juliet*

JULIET: Romeo!
ROMEO: It is my soul that calls upon my name!
How silver-sweet sound lovers' tongues by night,
Like softest music to attending ears.

If music be the food of love, play on

Orsino, *Twelfth Night*

If music be the food of love, play on,
Give me excess of it, that, surfeiting,
The appetite may sicken, and so die.
That strain again! It had a dying fall.
Oh, it came o'er my ear like the sweet sound
That breathes upon a bank of violets,
Stealing and giving odour. Enough, no more,
'Tis not so sweet now as it was before.

The barge she sat in, like a burnished throne

Enobarbus, *Antony and Cleopatra*

The barge she sat in, like a burnished throne,
Burned on the water. The poop was beaten gold,
Purple the sails, and so perfumed that
The winds were love-sick with them; the oars were
silver,
Which to the tune of flutes kept stroke, and made
The water which they beat to follow faster,
As amorous of their strokes. For her own person,
It beggared all description.

Who is Silvia? What is she?

Song, *Two Gentlemen of Verona*

Who is Silvia? What is she?
  That all our swains commend her?
Holy, fair, and wise is she,
  The heaven such grace did lend her,
That she might admired be.

Is she kind as she is fair?
  For beauty lives with kindness.
Love doth to her eyes repair,
  To help him of his blindness,
And, being helped, inhabits there.

Then to Silvia let us sing,
  That Silvia is excelling.
She excels each mortal thing
  Upon the dull earth dwelling.
To her let us garlands bring.

An angel is like you, Kate, and you are like an angel

King Henry, *Henry V*

HENRY: Fair Katherine, and most fair,
Will you vouchsafe to teach a soldier terms
Such as will enter at a lady's ear
And plead his love-suit to her gentle heart?

KATE: Your majesty shall mock at me; I cannot speak your England.

HENRY: O fair Katherine, if you will love me soundly with your French heart I will be glad to hear you confess it brokenly with your English tongue. Do you like me, Kate?

KATE: Pardonnez-moi, I cannot tell vat is "like me".

HENRY: An angel is like you, Kate, and you are like an angel.

The fair, the chaste, and unexpressive she

Orlando, *As You Like It*

Hang there, my verse, in witness of my love,
And thou, thrice-crowned queen of night, survey
With thy chaste eye, from thy pale sphere above,
Thy huntress' name that my full life doth sway.
O Rosalind, these trees shall be my books,
And in their barks my thoughts I'll character,
That every eye which in this forest looks
Shall see thy virtue witnessed everywhere.
Run, run, Orlando, carve on every tree
The fair, the chaste, and unexpressive she.

Was ever woman in this humour wooed?

King Richard, *Richard III*

Was ever woman in this humour wooed?
Was ever woman in this humour won?
I'll have her, but I will not keep her long.
What? I that killed her husband and his father,
To take her in her heart's extremest hate,
With curses in her mouth, tears in her eyes,
The bleeding witness of her hatred by,
Having God, her conscience, and these bars against me,
And I, no friends to back my suit at all,
But the plain devil and dissembling looks –
And yet to win her, all the world to nothing! Ha!

I do love nothing in the world so well as you

Benedick, *Much Ado About Nothing*

BENEDICK: I do love nothing in the world so well as you – is not that strange?

BEATRICE: As strange as the thing I know not. It were as possible for me to say I loved nothing so well as you, but believe me not; and yet I lie not; I confess nothing, nor I deny nothing. I am sorry for my cousin.

BENEDICK: By my sword, Beatrice, thou lovest me.

BEATRICE: Do not swear and eat it.

BENEDICK: I will swear by it that you love me, and I will make him eat it that says I love not you.

BEATRICE: Will you not eat your word?

BENEDICK: With no sauce that can be devised to it. I protest I love thee.

BEATRICE: Why then, God forgive me.

BENEDICK: What offence, sweet Beatrice?

BEATRICE: You have stayed me in a happy hour. I was about to protest I loved you.

BENEDICK: And do it with all thy heart.

BEATRICE: I love you with so much of my heart that none is left to protest.

BENEDICK: Come, bid me do anything for thee.

BEATRICE: Kill Claudio.

Blood, thou art blood

Angelo, *Measure for Measure*

When I would pray and think, I think and pray
To several subjects. Heaven hath my empty words,
Whilst my invention, hearing not my tongue,
Anchors on Isabel; Heaven in my mouth,
As if I did but only chew his name,
And in my heart the strong and swelling evil
Of my conception. The state whereon I studied
Is, like a good thing being often read,
Grown sere and tedious. Yea, my gravity,
Wherein – let no man hear me – I take pride,
Could I with boot change for an idle plume
Which the air beats for vain. O place, O form,
How often dost thou with thy case, thy habit,
Wrench awe from fools, and tie the wiser souls
To thy false seeming! Blood, thou art blood.

That I should love a bright particular star

Helena, *All's Well That Ends Well*

I think not on my father,
And these great tears grace his remembrance more
Than those I shed for him. What was he like?
I have forgot him. My imagination
Carries no favour in't but Bertram's.
I am undone. There is no living, none,
If Bertram be away. 'Twere all one
That I should love a bright particular star
And think to wed it, he is so above me.
In his bright radiance and collateral light
Must I be comforted, not in his sphere.

O, swear not by the moon

Juliet, *Romeo and Juliet*

ROMEO: Lady, by yonder blessed moon I swear
That tips with silver all these fruit-tree tops –
JULIET: O, swear not by the moon, the inconstant moon,
That monthly changes in her circled orb,
Lest that thy love prove likewise variable.

As woman's love

Prince Hamlet, *Hamlet*

HAMLET: Is this a prologue, or the posy of a ring?
OPHELIA: 'Tis brief, my lord.
HAMLET: As woman's love.

Sigh no more, ladies, sigh no more

Balthasar's Song, *Much Ado About Nothing*

Sigh no more, ladies, sigh no more.
  Men were deceivers ever,
One foot in the sea, and one on shore,
  To one thing constant never.
Then sigh not so, but let them go,
  And be you blithe and bonny,
Converting all your sounds of woe
  Into hey nonny nonny.

Sing no more ditties, sing no more
  Of dumps so dull and heavy.
The fraud of men was ever so
  Since summer first was leafy.
Then sigh not so, but let them go,
  And be you blithe and bonny,
Converting all your sounds of woe
  Into hey nonny nonny.

The moated grange

Duke, *Measure for Measure*

There at the moated grange resides this dejected Mariana.

Rich gifts wax poor when givers prove unkind

Ophelia, *Hamlet*

OPHELIA: My lord, I have remembrances of yours
That I have longed long to redeliver.
I pray you now, receive them.
HAMLET: No, no, I never gave you aught.
OPHELIA: My honoured lord, you know right well you did,
And with them words of so sweet breath composed
As made the things more rich. Their perfume lost,
Take these again; for to the noble mind
Rich gifts wax poor when givers prove unkind.

A fickle maid full pale

A Lover's Complaint

From off a hill whose concave womb re-worded
A plaintful story from a sist'ring vale,
My spirits t'attend this double voice accorded,
And down I laid to list the sad-tuned tale;
Ere long espied a fickle maid full pale,
Tearing of papers, breaking rings a-twain,
Storming her world with sorrow's wind and rain.

The poor soul sat sighing by a sycamore tree

Desdemona's Song, *Othello*

The poor soul sat sighing by a sycamore tree,
  Sing all a green willow.
Her hand on her bosom, her head on her knee,
  Sing willow, willow, willow.
The fresh streams ran by her and murmured her moans,
  Sing willow, willow, willow,
Her salt tears fell from her, and softened the stones,
  Sing willow, willow, willow,
Sing all, a green willow must be my garland.

The course of true love never did run smooth

Lysander, *A Midsummer Night's Dream*

Ay me, for aught that I could ever read,
Could ever hear by tale or history,
The course of true love never did run smooth.

Men have died . . . but not for love

Rosalind, *As You Like It*

The poor world is almost six thousand years old, and in all this time there was not any man died in his own person, in a love-cause.

Troilus had his brains dashed out with a Grecian club, yet he did what he could to die before, and he is one of the patterns of love.

Leander, he would have lived many a fair year though Hero had turned nun, if it had not been for a hot midsummer night; for, good youth, he went forth to wash him in the Hellespont, and being taken with the cramp, was drowned, and the foolish chroniclers of that age found it was Hero of Sestos.

But these are all lies: men have died from time to time and worms have eaten them, but not for love.

Thus with a kiss I die

Romeo in Juliet's tomb, *Romeo and Juliet*

Ah, dear Juliet,
Why art thou yet so fair? Shall I believe
That unsubstantial Death is amorous
And that the lean abhorred monster keeps
Thee here in dark to be his paramour?
For fear of that I still will stay with thee,
And never from this palace of dim night
Depart again. Here, here will I remain
With worms that are thy chambermaids. O here
Will I set up my everlasting rest,
And shake the yoke of inauspicious stars
From this world-wearied flesh. Eyes, look your last.
Arms, take your last embrace, and lips – O you
The doors of breath! – seal with a righteous kiss
A dateless bargain to engrossing Death.
Come, bitter conduct, come, unsavoury guide,
Thou desperate pilot, now at once run on
The dashing rocks thy seasick weary bark!
Here's to my love! O true apothecary,
Thy drugs are quick! Thus with a kiss I die.

Now die, die, die, die, die.

Bottom, in the part of Pyramus,
A Midsummer Night's Dream

"O wherefore, nature, didst thou lions frame,
Since lion vile hath here deflowered my dear?
Which is" – no, no – "Which was the fairest dame
That lived, that loved, that liked, that looked, with cheer?
Come, tears, confound! Out, sword, and wound
The pap of Pyramus!
Ay, that left pap, where heart doth hop.
Thus die I: thus, thus, thus, thus!
Now am I dead! Now am I fled!
My soul is in the sky!
Tongue lose thy light!
Moon take thy flight!
Now die, die, die, die, die."

I have railed so long against marriage . . .

Benedick, *Much Ado About Nothing*

I may chance have some odd quirks and remnants of wit broken on me because I have railed so long against marriage. But doth not the appetite alter? A man loves the meat in his youth that he cannot endure in his age. Shall quips and sentences and these paper bullets of the brain awe a man from the career of his humour? No. The world must be peopled. When I said I would die a bachelor, I did not think I should live till I were married.

Withering on the virgin thorn

Theseus, *A Midsummer Night's Dream*

HERMIA: But I beseech your grace that I may know
The worst that may befall me in this case
If I refuse to wed Demetrius.
THESEUS: Either to die the death, or to abjure
For ever the society of men.
Therefore, fair Hermia, question your desires.
Know of your youth, examine well your blood,
Whether, if you yield not to your father's choice,
You can endure the livery of a nun,
For aye to be in shady cloister mewed,
To live a barren sister all your life,
Chanting fair hymns to the cold fruitless moon,
Thrice blessed they that master so their blood
To undergo such maiden pilgrimage;
But earthlier happy, is the rose distilled
Than that which, withering on the virgin thorn,
Grows, lives, and dies in single blessedness.

Get thee to a nunnery!

Prince Hamlet, *Hamlet*

If thou dost marry, I'll give thee this plague for thy dowry: be thou as chaste as ice, as pure as snow, thou shalt not escape calumny. Get thee to a nunnery! Farewell. Or if thou wilt needs marry, marry a fool; for wise men know well enough what monsters you make of them. To a nunnery, go – and quickly too. Farewell.

And will you, nill you, I will marry you

Petruchio, *The Taming of the Shrew*

Marry, so I mean, sweet Katherine, in thy bed.
And therefore, setting all this chat aside,
Thus in plain terms: your father hath consented
That you shall be my wife; your dowry 'greed on;
And will you, nill you, I will marry you.
Now, Kate, I am a husband for your turn,
For by this light, whereby I see thy beauty,
Thy beauty that doth make me like thee well,
Thou must be married to no man but me.
For I am born to tame you, Kate,
And bring you from a wild Kate to a Kate
Conformable as other household Kates.

Kiss me, Kate

Petruchio, *The Taming of the Shrew*

PETRUCHIO: Kiss me, Kate, we will be married o' Sunday!
GREMIO: Was ever match clapped up so suddenly?

Whiles a wedlock hymn we sing

Hymen, *As You Like It*

Peace, ho! I bar confusion
'Tis I must make conclusion
Of these most strange events.
Here's eight that must take hands
To join in Hymen's bands,
If truth holds true contents.
You and you no cross shall part.
You and you are heart and heart.
You to his love must accord,
Or have a woman to your lord.
You and you are sure together
As the winter to foul weather.
Whiles a wedlock hymn we sing,
Feed yourselves with questioning,
That reason wonder may diminish
How thus we met, and these things finish.
Wedding is great Juno's crown,
O blessed bond of board and bed.
'Tis Hymen peoples every town.
High wedlock then be honoured.
Honour, high honour and renown,
To Hymen, god of every town.

One mutual happiness

Valentine, *Two Gentlemen of Verona*

That done, our day of marriage shall be yours,
One feast, one house, one mutual happiness.

Jack shall have Jill

Puck, *A Midsummer Night's Dream*

Jack shall have Jill.
Naught shall go ill,
The man shall have his mare again,
And all shall be well.

Hanging and wiving goes by destiny

Nerissa, *The Merchant of Venice*

The ancient saying is no heresy,
Hanging and wiving goes by destiny.

The marriage of true minds

Sonnet 116

Let me not to the marriage of true minds
Admit impediment. Love is not love
Which alters when it alteration finds,
Or bends with the remover to remove.
Oh no, it is an ever-fixed mark,
That looks on tempests and is never shaken.
It is the star to every wand'ring bark,
Whose worth's unknown, although his height be taken.
Love's not Time's fool, though rosy lips and cheeks
Within his bending sickle's compass come.
Love alters not with his brief hours and weeks,
But bears it out even to the edge of doom.
If this be error and upon me proved,
I never writ, nor no man ever loved.

As the ox hath his bow

Jaques, *As You Like It*

JAQUES: Will you be married, motley?
TOUCHSTONE: As the ox hath his bow, sir, the horse his curb, and the falcon her bells, so man hath his desires, and as the pigeons bill, so wedlock would be nibbling.

And when I love thee not

Othello, *Othello*

Excellent wretch! Perdition catch my soul
But I do love thee! and when I love thee not,
Chaos is come again.

Do you not love me? Do you not indeed?

Kate, wife to Hotspur, *Henry IV, Part One*

KATE: Come, come, you paraquito, answer me
Directly to this question that I ask.
In faith, I'll break thy little finger, Harry,
An if thou wilt not tell me all things true.
HOTSPUR: Away, you trifler! Love? I love thee not,
I care not for thee, Kate. This is no world
To play with mammets, and to tilt with lips;
We must have bloody noses, and cracked crowns,
And pass them current too – God's me! My horse!
What say'st thou, Kate? What wouldst thou have with
me?
KATE: Do you not love me? Do you not indeed?
Well, do not then, for since you love me not
I will not love myself. Do you not love me?
Nay, tell me if you speak in jest or no.
HOTSPUR: Come, wilt thou see me ride?
And when I am a horseback, I will swear
I love thee infinitely.

I am not Adriana, nor thy wife

Adriana, *The Comedy of Errors*

Ay, ay, Antipholus, look strange and frown,
Some other mistress hath thy sweet aspects.
I am not Adriana, nor thy wife.
The time was once when thou unurged wouldst vow
That never words were music to thine ear,
That never object pleasing to thine eye,
That never touch well welcome to thy hand,
That never meat sweet-savoured in thy taste,
Unless I spake, or looked, or touched, or carved to thee.
How comes it now, my husband, O how comes it,
That thou art then estranged from thyself?

What a falling off was there!

Ghost, *Hamlet*

O Hamlet, what a falling off was there!
From me, whose love was of that dignity
That it went hand-in-hand even with the vow
I made to her in marriage – and to decline
Upon a wretch whose natural gifts were poor
To those of mine!

Dwell I but in the suburbs of your good pleasure?

Portia, *Julius Caesar*

BRUTUS: Kneel not, gentle Portia.
PORTIA: I should not need if you were gentle, Brutus.
Within the bond of marriage, tell me, Brutus,
Is it excepted I should know no secrets
That appertain to you? Am I your self
But, as it were, in sort or limitation,
To keep with you at meals, comfort your bed,
And talk to you sometimes? Dwell I but in the suburbs
Of your good pleasure? If it be no more,
Portia is Brutus' harlot, not his wife.
BRUTUS: You are my true and honourable wife,
As dear to me as are the ruddy drops
That visit my sad heart.

Let husbands know

Emilia, *Othello*

  Let husbands know
Their wives have sense like them: they see, and smell,
And have their palates both for sweet and sour,
As husbands have. What is it that they do,
When they change us for others? Is it sport?
I think it is: and doth affection breed it?
I think it doth. Is't frailty that thus errs?
It is so too. And have we not affections,
Desires for sport, and frailty, as men have?
Then let them use us well: else let them know
The ills we do, their ills instruct us so.

Ill met by moonlight, proud Titania

Oberon, *A Midsummer Night's Dream*

OBERON: Ill met by moonlight, proud Titania.
TITANIA: What, jealous Oberon? Fairies, skip hence;
I have forsworn his bed and company.
OBERON: Tarry, rash wanton. Am I not your lord?
TITANIA: Then I must be thy lady. But I know
When thou hast stol'n away from fairy land,
And in the shape of Corin, sat all day
Playing on pipes of corn, and versing love
To amorous Phillida.

Is whispering nothing?

Leontes, *The Winter's Tale*

Is whispering nothing?
Is leaning cheek to cheek? Is meeting noses?
Kissing with inside lip? Stopping the career
Of laughter with a sigh? – a note infallible
Of breaking honesty! – Horsing foot on foot?
Skulking in corners? Wishing clocks more swift,
Hours minutes, noon midnight? And all eyes
Blind with the pin and web but theirs, theirs only,
That would unseen be wicked? Is this nothing?
Why then the world and all that's in't is nothing!
The covering sky is nothing, Bohemia is nothing,
My wife is nothing, nor nothing have these nothings
If this be nothing.

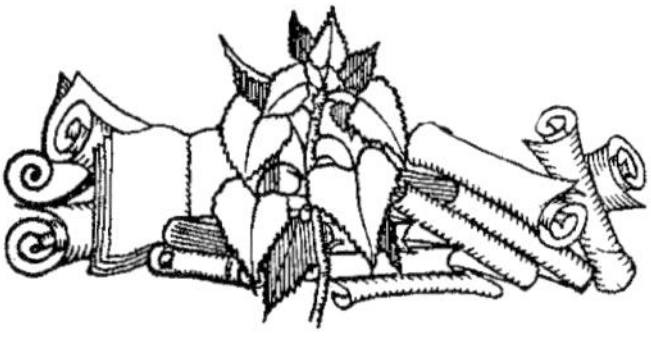

Let's have one other gaudy night

Antony, *Antony and Cleopatra*

ANTONY: Come,
Let's have one other gaudy night. Call to me
All my sad captains. Fill our bowls once more.
Let's mock the midnight bell.
CLEOPATRA: It is my birthday.
I had thought to've held it poor, but since my lord
Is Antony again, I will be Cleopatra.
ANTONY: We will yet do well.

We have beat them to their beds

Antony, *Antony and Cleopatra*

CLEOPATRA: Lord of lords,
O infinite virtue, com'st thou smiling from
The world's great snare uncaught?
ANTONY: My nightingale,
We have beat them to their beds. What, girl? Though grey
Do something mingle with our younger brown, yet ha' we
A brain that nourishes our nerves, and can
Get goal for goal of youth!

Do not speak like a death's-head

Doll Tearsheet, *Henry IV, Part Two*

DOLL: Thou whoreson little tidy Bartholomew boar-pig, when wilt thou leave fighting a-days, and foining a-nights, and begin to patch up thine old body for heaven?

FALSTAFF: Peace, good Doll, do not speak like a death's-head, do not bid me remember mine end.

Saturn and Venus this year in conjunction!

Prince Hal, *Henry IV, Part Two*

POINS: Let's beat him before his whore.
HAL: Look whe'er the withered elder hath not his poll clawed like a parrot!
POINS: Is it not strange that desire should so many years outlive performance?
FALSTAFF: Kiss me, Doll.
HAL: Saturn and Venus this year in conjunction!

Journeys end in lovers' meeting

Feste's Song, *Twelfth Night*

O mistress mine, where are you roaming?
O stay and hear, your true love's coming,
  That can sing both high and low.
Trip no further, pretty sweeting.
Journeys end in lovers' meeting,
  Every wise man's son doth know.

I will encounter darkness as a bride

Claudio, *Measure for Measure*

If I must die,
I will encounter darkness as a bride,
And hug it in mine arms.

~

My second best bed

Shakespeare's will, 1616

Item, I give unto my wife my second best bed, with the furniture.

Chapter 4

SALAD DAYS AND SNOW BROTH

In Shakespeare's time, New Year's Day fell not on 1 January but on 25 March. His drama, like the calendar year, was intimately attuned to the natural cycle of the seasons, as the titles of his Twelfth Night, A Midsummer Night's Dream, *or* A Winter's Tale *show. "One, two, three. Time, time!" (Iachimo,* Cymbeline*).*

When daisies pied and violets blue

Song of Spring, *Love's Labour's Lost*

When daisies pied and violets blue
  And lady-smocks all silver-white
And cuckoo-buds of yellow hue
  Do paint the meadows with delight,
The cuckoo then on every tree
Mocks married men, for thus sings he,
  Cuckoo!
Cuckoo, cuckoo! O word of fear,
Unpleasing to a married ear!

When shepherds pipe on oaten straws,
  And merry larks are ploughmen's clocks,
When turtles tread, and rooks, and daws,
  And maidens bleach their summer smocks,
The cuckoo then on every tree
Mocks married men, for thus sings he,
  Cuckoo!
Cuckoo, cuckoo! O word of fear,
Unpleasing to a married ear!

Beware the ides of March

Soothsayer, *Julius Caesar*

CAESAR: What sayst thou to me now? Speak once again.
SOOTHSAYER: Beware the ides of March.
CAESAR: He is a dreamer. Let us leave him. Pass.

Daffodils, that come before the swallow dares

Perdita, *The Winter's Tale*

Daffodils,
That come before the swallow dares, and take
The winds of March with beauty; violets, dim
But sweeter than the lids of Juno's eyes
Or Cytherea's breath; pale primroses
That die unmarried; ere they can behold
Bright Phoebus in his strength.

Salad days

Cleopatra, *Antony and Cleopatra*

My salad days,
When I was green in judgement, cold in blood,
To say as I said then.

Sweet lovers love the spring

Song, *As You Like It*

It was a lover and his lass,
  With a hey, and a ho, and a hey-nonny-no,
That o'er the green cornfield did pass,
  In the spring time, the only pretty ring time,
When birds do sing, hey-ding-a-ding;
Sweet lovers love the spring.

Between the acres of the rye,
  With a hey, and a ho, and a hey-nonny-no,
These pretty country folks would lie,
  In the spring time, the only pretty ring time,
When birds do sing, hey-ding-a-ding;
Sweet lovers love the spring.

This carol they began that hour,
  With a hey, and a ho, and a hey-nonny-no,
How that a life was but a flower,
  In the spring time, the only pretty ring time,
When birds do sing, hey-ding-a-ding;
Sweet lovers love the spring.

And therefore take the present time,
  With a hey, and a ho, and a hey-nonny-no,
For love is crowned with the prime,
  In the spring time, the only pretty ring time,
When birds do sing, hey-ding-a-ding;
Sweet lovers love the spring.

The ides of March are come

Caesar, *Julius Caesar*

CAESAR: The ides of March are come.
SOOTHSAYER: Ay, Caesar, but not gone.

From you have I been absent in the spring

Sonnet 98

From you have I been absent in the spring
When proud-pied April, dressed in all his trim,
Hath put a spirit of youth in everything.

~

The uncertain glory of an April day

Proteus, *The Two Gentlemen of Verona*

O, how this spring of love resembleth
The uncertain glory of an April day,
Which now shows all the beauty of the sun,
And by and by a cloud takes all away.

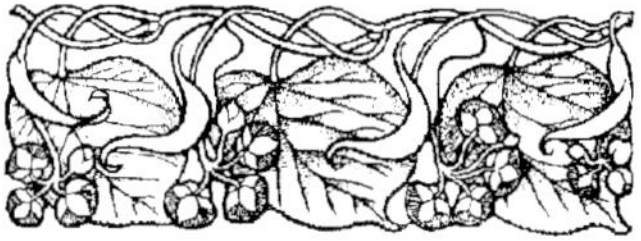

Men are April when they woo

Rosalind, *As You Like It*

Men are April when they woo, December when they wed. Maids are May when they are maids, but the sky changes when they are wives. I will be more jealous of thee than a Barbary cock-pigeon over his hen, more clamorous than a parrot against rain, more new-fangled than an ape, more giddy in my desires than a monkey.

Fresher than May

Arcite, *The Two Noble Kinsmen*

O Queen Emilia,
Fresher than May, sweeter
Than her gold buttons on the bough, or all
Th' enamelled knacks o' th' mead or garden – yea,
We challenge too the bank of any nymph
That makes the stream seem flowers – thou, O jewel
O' th' wood, hast likewise blessed a place
With thy sole presence.

The quality of mercy is not strained

Portia, *The Merchant of Venice*

The quality of mercy is not strained,
It droppeth as the gentle rain from heaven
Upon the place beneath: it is twice blessed,
It blesseth him that gives, and him that takes,
'Tis mightiest in the mightiest, it becomes
The throned monarch better than his crown.

~

Sunshine and rain at once

Gentleman, *King Lear*

KENT: Oh, then it moved her?
GENT: Not to a rage. Patience and sorrow strove
Who should express her goodliest. You have seen
Sunshine and rain at once? Her smiles and tears
Were like, a better way: those happy smilets
That played on her ripe lip seemed not to know
What guests were in her eyes; which parted thence,
As pearls from diamonds dropped.

The third day comes a frost, a killing frost

Cardinal Wolsey, *Henry VIII*

This is the state of man. Today he puts forth
The tender leaves of hopes; tomorrow blossoms,
And bears his blushing honours thick upon him:
The third day comes a frost, a killing frost,
And when he thinks, good easy man, full surely
His greatness is a-ripening, nips his root,
And then falls as I do. I have ventured
Like little wanton boys that swim on bladders,
This many summers in a sea of glory,
But far beyond my depth.

And hang a pearl in every cowslip's ear

Fairy's Song, *A Midsummer Night's Dream*

Over hill, over dale,
  Thorough bush, thorough briar,
Over park, over pale,
  Thorough flood, thorough fire,
I do wander everywhere,
Swifter than the moon's sphere;
And I serve the Fairy Queen,
To dew her orbs upon the green.
The cowslips tall her pensioners be,
In their gold coats spots you see:
Those be rubies, fairy favours,
In those freckles live their savours.
I must go seek some dew-drops here,
And hang a pearl in every cowslip's ear.

Shall I compare thee to a summer's day?

Sonnet 18

Shall I compare thee to a summer's day?
Thou art more lovely and more temperate.
Rough winds do shake the darling buds of May,
And summer's lease hath all too short a date.
Sometimes too hot the eye of heaven shines,
And often is his gold complexion dimmed;
And every fair from fair sometime declines,
By chance or nature's changing course untrimmed.
But thy eternal summer shall not fade,
Nor lose possession of that fair thou ow'st,
Nor shall death brag thou wander'st in his shade
When in eternal lines to time thou grow'st:
So long as men can breathe or eyes can see,
So long lives this, and this gives life to thee.

Why then comes in the sweet o' the year

Autolycus, *The Winter's Tale*

When daffodils begin to peer,
  With hey, the doxy over the dale,
Why then comes in the sweet o' the year,
  For the red blood reigns in the winter's pale.

The white sheet bleaching on the hedge,
  With hey, the sweet birds, O how they sing!
Doth set my pugging tooth on edge,
  For a quart of ale is a dish for a king.

The lark, that tirra-lirra chants,
  With hey, with hey, the thrush and the jay,
Are summer songs for me and my aunts
  While we lie tumbling in the hay.

I know a bank where the wild thyme blows

Oberon, *A Midsummer Night's Dream*

I know a bank where the wild thyme blows,
Where oxlips and the nodding violet grows,
Quite over-canopied with luscious woodbine,
With sweet musk-roses and with eglantine.
There sleeps Titania sometime of the night,
Lulled in these flowers with dances and delight;
And there the snake throws her enamelled skin,
Weed wide enough to wrap a fairy in.

Now is the winter of our discontent

King Richard, *Richard III*

Now is the winter of our discontent
Made glorious summer by this son of York,
And all the clouds that loured upon our house
In the deep bosom of the ocean buried.

In such a night as this

Lorenzo, *The Merchant of Venice*

The moon shines bright. In such a night as this,
When the sweet wind did gently kiss the trees,
And they did make no noise, in such a night
Troilus, methinks, mounted the Trojan walls
And sighed his soul toward the Grecian tents
Where Cressid lay that night.

Full many a glorious morning have I seen

Sonnet 35

Full many a glorious morning have I seen
Flatter the mountain-tops with sovereign eye,
Kissing with golden face the meadows green,
Gilding pale streams with heavenly alchemy.

Yet herein will I imitate the sun

Prince Hal, *Henry IV, Part One*

I know you all, and will a while uphold
The unyoked humour of your idleness.
Yet herein will I imitate the sun,
Who doth permit the base contagious clouds
To smother up his beauty from the world,
That, when he please again to be himself,
Being wanted he may be more wondered at
By breaking through the foul and ugly mists
Of vapours that did seem to strangle him.
If all the year were playing holidays,
To sport would be as tedious as to work.

Shine out, fair sun

King Richard, *Richard III*

Shine out, fair sun, till I have bought a glass,
That I may see my shadow as I pass.

Like a cow in June

Scarus, *Antony and Cleopatra*

Yon riband-red nag of Egypt –
Whom leprosy o'ertake! – i' th' midst o' th' fight,
When vantage like a pair of twins appeared,
Both as the same, or rather ours the elder
The breeze upon her, like a cow in June,
Hoists sails and flies.

My mistress' eyes are nothing like the sun

Sonnet 130

My mistress' eyes are nothing like the sun;
Coral is far more red than her lips' red.
If snow be white, why then her breasts be dun;
If hairs be wires, black wires grow on her head.

Fear no more the heat of the sun

Song of Guiderius and Arviragus, *Cymbeline*

Fear no more the heat of the sun,
  Nor the furious winter's rages.
Thou thy worldly task has done,
  Home art gone and ta'en thy wages.
Golden lads and girls all must
As chimney-sweepers, come to dust.

Fear no more the frown of the great,
  Thou art past the tyrant's stroke.
Care no more to clothe and eat,
  To thee the reed is as the oak:
The sceptre, learning, physic, must
All follow this and come to dust.

Fear no more the lightning-flash.
  Nor th'all-dreaded thunder-stone.
Fear not slander, censure rash.
  Thou hast finished joy and moan.
All lovers young, all lovers must
Consign to thee and come to dust.

Ah what a life were this! How sweet, how lovely!

King Henry, *Henry VI, Part Three*

Ah what a life were this! How sweet, how lovely!
Gives not the hawthorn bush a sweeter shade
To shepherds looking on their silly sheep
Than doth a rich embroidered canopy
To kings that fear their subjects' treachery?
O yes, it doth, a thousand-fold it doth.
And to conclude, the shepherd's homely curds,
His cold thin drink out of his leather bottle,
His wonted sleep under a fresh tree's shade,
All which secure and sweetly he enjoys,
Is far beyond a prince's delicates –
His viands sparkling in a golden cup,
His body couched in a curious bed –
When Care, Mistrust and Treason waits on him.

Earth's increase and foison plenty

Ceres' Song, *The Tempest*

Earth's increase and foison plenty,
Barns and garners never empty,
Vines with clust'ring bunches growing,
Plants with goodly burden bowing.
Spring come to you at the farthest,
In the very end of harvest.
Scarcity and want shall shun you,
Ceres' blessing so is on you.

Go, bind thou up yon dangling apricots

The Gardener, *Richard II*

Go, bind thou up yon dangling apricots,
Which, like unruly children, make their sire
Stoop with oppression of their prodigal weight.
Give some supportance to the bending twigs.
Go thou, and like an executioner,
Cut off the heads of too fast-growing sprays
That look too lofty in our commonwealth:
All must be even in our government.
You thus employed, I will go root away
The noisome weeds which without profit suck
The soil's fertility, from wholesome flowers.

All her husbandry doth lie on heaps

Burgundy, *Henry V*

Alas, she hath from France too long been chased,
And all her husbandry doth lie on heaps,
Corrupting in it own fertility.
Her vine, the merry cheerer of the heart,
Unpruned dies; her hedges even-pleached,
Like prisoners wildly overgrown with hair,
Put forth disordered twigs; her fallow leas
The darnel, hemlock and rank fumitory
Doth root upon, while that the coulter rusts
That should deracinate such savagery.
The even mead – that erst brought sweetly forth
The freckled cowslip, burnet and green clover -
Wanting the scythe, all uncorrected, rank,
Conceives by idleness, and nothing teems,
But hateful docks, rough thistles, kecksies, burs,
Losing both beauty and utility.

That time of year thou mayst in me behold

Sonnet 73

That time of year thou mayst in me behold,
When yellow leaves, or none, or few, do hang
Upon these boughs which shake against the cold,
Bare ruined choirs where late the sweet birds sang.

The sear, the yellow leaf

Macbeth, *Macbeth*

I have lived long enough: my way of life
Is fall'n into the sear, the yellow leaf.

Valiant foemen, like to autumn's corn

King Edward, *Henry VI Part Three*

Once more we sit in England's royal throne,
Repurchased with the blood of enemies.
What valiant foemen, like to autumn's corn,
Have we mowed down in tops of all their pride!

There is a willow grows aslant a brook

Gertrude, *Hamlet*

There is a willow grows aslant a brook
That shows his hoary leaves in the glassy stream.
Therewith fantastic garlands did she make
Of crow-flowers, nettles, daisies and long purples,
That liberal shepherds give a grosser name,
But our cold maids "dead men's fingers" call them.
There on the pendent boughs her crownet weeds
Clamb'ring to hang, an envious sliver broke,
When down her weedy trophies and herself
Fell in the weeping brook. Her clothes spread wide,
And mermaid-like awhile they bore her up;
Which time she chanted snatches of old tunes,
As one incapable of her own distress,
Or like a creature native and endued
Unto that element. But long it could not be
Till that her garments, heavy with their drink,
Pulled the poor wretch from her melodious lay
To muddy death.

The nine men's morris is filled up with mud

Titania, *A Midsummer Night's Dream*

Therefore the winds, piping to us in vain,
As in revenge have sucked up from the sea
Contagious fogs, which, falling in the land,
Hath every pelting river made so proud
That they have overborne their continents.
The ox hath therefore stretched his yoke in vain,
The ploughman lost his sweat, and the green corn
Hath rotted ere his youth attained a beard.
The fold stands empty in the drowned field,
And crows are fatted with the murrain flock.
The nine men's morris is filled up with mud,
And the quaint mazes in the wanton green
For lack of tread are undistinguishable.

For the rain it raineth every day

Feste's Song, *Twelfth Night*

When that I was and a little tiny boy,
  With hey, ho, the wind and the rain;
A foolish thing was but a toy,
  For the rain it raineth every day.

But when I came to man's estate,
  With hey, ho, the wind and the rain,
'Gainst knaves and thieves men shut their gate,
  For the rain it raineth every day.

But when I came, alas, to wive,
  With hey, ho, the wind and the rain,
By swaggering could I never thrive,
  For the rain it raineth every day.

A great while ago the world begun,
  With hey ho, the wind and the rain,
But that's all one, our play is done,
  For the rain it raineth every day.

When shall we three meet again?

First Witch, *Macbeth*

FIRST WITCH: When shall we three meet again?
In thunder, lightning or in rain?
SECOND WITCH: When the hurlyburly's done,
When the battle's lost and won.
THIRD WITCH: That will be ere the set of sun.
FIRST WITCH: Where the place?
SECOND WITCH: Upon the heath.
THIRD WITCH: There to meet with Macbeth.
FIRST WITCH: I come, Graymalkin!
SECOND WITCH: Paddock calls.
THIRD WITCH: Anon!
ALL: Fair is foul, and foul is fair:
Hover through the filthy air.

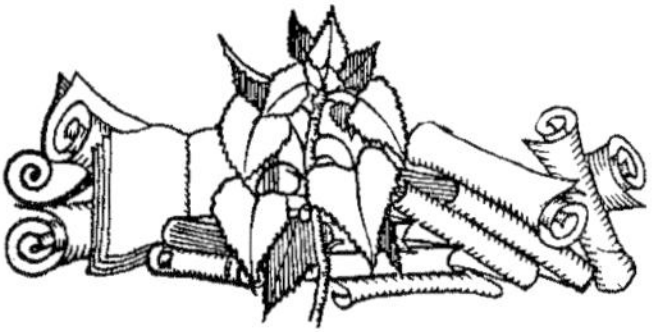

Blow winds and crack your cheeks!

Lear, *King Lear*

Blow winds and crack your cheeks! Rage, blow,
You cataracts and hurricanoes, spout
Till you have drenched our steeples, drowned the cocks!
You sulph'rous and thought-executing fires,
Vaunt-couriers of oak-cleaving thuderbolts,
Singe my white head! And thou, all-shaking thunder,
Strike flat the thick rotundity o' th' world!
Crack nature's moulds, all germens spill at once
That makes ingrateful man!

Yet it shall be tempest-tossed

First Witch, *Macbeth*

Weary se'nnights nine times nine
Shall he dwindle, peak and pine.
Though his bark cannot be lost,
Yet it shall be tempest-tossed.

The sky, it seems, would pour down stinking pitch

Miranda, *The Tempest*

If by your art, my dearest father, you have
Put the wild waters in this roar, allay them.
The sky, it seems, would pour down stinking pitch,
But that the sea, mounting to th' welkin's cheek,
Dashes the fire out. Oh, I have suffered
With those that I saw suffer! A brave vessel,
Who had, no doubt, some noble creature in her,
Dashed all to pieces! Oh, the cry did knock
Against my very heart! Poor souls, they perished.
Had I been any god of power, I would
Have sunk the sea within the earth, or ere
It should the good ship so have swallowed and
The fraughting souls within her.

The pelting of this pitiless storm

Lear, *King Lear*

Poor naked wretches, whereso'er you are,
That bide the pelting of this pitiless storm,
How shall your houseless heads and unfed sides,
Your looped and windowed raggedness, defend you
From seasons such as these? O, I have ta'en
Too little care of this. Take physic, pomp,
Expose thyself to feel what wretches feel,
That thou mayst shake the superflux to them
And show the heavens more just.

For this relief much thanks

Francisco, *Hamlet*

BARNARDO: 'Tis now struck twelve. Get thee to bed, Francisco.
FRANCISCO: For this relief much thanks. 'Tis bitter cold
And I am sick at heart.

How like a winter hath my absence been

Sonnet 97

How like a winter hath my absence been
From thee, the pleasure of the fleeting year.
What freezings have I felt, what dark days seen,
What old December's bareness everywhere!

Or wallow naked in December snow

Bolingbroke, *Richard II*

GAUNT: What is six winters? They are quickly gone.
BOLINGBROKE: To men in joy but grief makes one hour ten.
GAUNT: Call it a travel that thou tak'st for pleasure.
BOLINGBROKE: My heart will sigh when I miscall it so,
Which finds it an enforced pilgrimage.
GAUNT: The sullen passage of thy weary steps
Esteem as foil wherein thou art to set
The precious jewel of thy home return.
BOLINGBROKE: Oh who can hold a fire in his hand
By thinking on the frosty Caucasus?
Or cloy the hungry edge of appetite
By bare imagination of a feast?
Or wallow naked in December snow
By thinking on fantastic summer's heat?
Oh no, the apprehension of the good
Gives but the greater feeling to the worse.

The rain and wind beat dark December

Arviragus, *Cymbeline*

What should we speak of
When we are old as you? When we shall hear
The rain and wind beat dark December, how,
In this our pinching cave, shall we discourse
The freezing hours away?

That winter lion

York, *Henry VI, Part Two*

Old Salisbury? Who can report of him,
That winter lion, who in rage forgets
Aged contusions, and all brush of time,
And like a gallant in the brow of youth,
Repairs him with occasion?

Sap-consuming winter's drizzled snow

Egeon, *The Comedy of Errors*

O Time's extremity,
Hast thou so cracked and splitted my poor tongue
In seven short years, that here my only son
Knows not my feeble key of untuned cares?
Though now this grained face of mine be hid
In sap-consuming winter's drizzled snow,
And all the conduits of my blood froze up,
Yet hath my night of life some memory;
My wasting lamps some fading glimmer left;
My dull deaf ears a little use to hear –
All these old witnesses, I cannot err,
Tell me thou art my son Antipholus.

Blow, blow, thou winter wind

Song, *As You Like It*

Blow, blow, thou winter wind,
Thou art not so unkind
  As man's ingratitude.
Thy tooth is not so keen,
Because thou art not seen,
  Although thy breath be rude.
Hey-ho, sing hey-ho, unto the green holly.
Most friendship is feigning, most loving mere folly.
  Then hey-ho, the holly,
  This life is most jolly.

Freeze, freeze, thou bitter sky,
Thou dost not bite so nigh
  As benefits forgot.
Though thou the waters warp,
Thy sting is not so sharp,
  As friend remembered not.
Hey-ho, sing hey-ho, unto the green holly
Most friendship is feigning, most loving mere folly.
  Then hey-ho, the holly,
  This life is most jolly.

A February face

Don Pedro, *Much Ado About Nothing*

Good morrow, Benedick. Why, what's the matter,
That you have such a February face,
So full of frost, of storm, and cloudiness?

Pity, like a naked new-born babe

Macbeth, *Macbeth*

And Pity, like a naked new-born babe,
Striding the blast, or heaven's cherubim, horsed
Upon the sightless couriers of the air,
Shall blow the horrid deed in every eye,
That tears shall drown the wind. I have no spur
To prick the sides of my intent, but only
Vaulting ambition, which o'erleaps itself
And falls on th' other.

O that I were a mockery king of snow

King Richard, *Richard II*

O that I were a mockery king of snow,
Standing before the sun of Bolingbroke,
To melt myself away in water-drops!

~

Snow broth

Lucio, *Measure for Measure*

Upon his place,
And with full line of his authority,
Governs Lord Angelo, a man whose blood
Is very snow broth.

~

A sad tale's best for winter

Mamillius, *The Winter's Tale*

A sad tale's best for winter.
I have one of sprites and goblins.

This tale of Herne the hunter

Mistress Page, *The Merry Wives of Windsor*

There is an old tale goes that Herne the hunter,
Sometime a keeper here in Windsor Forest,
Doth all the winter-time at still midnight,
Walk round about an oak, with great ragged horns,
And there he blasts the trees, and takes the cattle,
And makes milch-kine yield blood, and shakes a
chain
In a most hideous and dreadful manner.
You have heard of such a spirit, and well you know
The superstitious idle-headed eld
Received and did deliver to our age,
This tale of Herne the hunter for a truth.

For you, there's rosemary and rue

Perdita, *The Winter's Tale*

For you, there's rosemary and rue. These keep
Seeming and savour all the winter long.
Grace and remembrance to you both,
And welcome to our shearing.

His beard as white as snow

Ophelia's Song, *Hamlet*

And will he not come again,
And will he not come again?
  No, no, he is dead,
  Go to thy death-bed,
He never will come again.

His beard as white as snow,
All flaxen was his poll.
  He is gone, he is gone,
  And we cast away moan.
God 'a mercy on his soul.

The seasons alter

Titania, *A Midsummer Night's Dream*

The human mortals want their winter cheer,
No night is now with hymn or carol blessed.
Therefore the moon, the governess of floods,
Pale in her anger washes all the air,
That rheumatic diseases do abound;
And thorough this distemperature we see
The seasons alter. Hoary-headed frosts
Fall in the fresh lap of the crimson rose,
And on old Hiems' thin and icy crown
An odorous chaplet of sweet summer buds
Is, as in mock'ry, set. The spring, the summer,
The childing autumn, angry winter change
Their wonted liveries, and the 'mazed world
By their increase now knows not which is which.

O earth, I will befriend thee more with rain

Titus, *Titus Andronicus*

O earth, I will befriend thee more with rain
That shall distil from these two ancient ruins
Than youthful April shall with all his showers.
In summer's drought I'll drop upon thee still.
In winter with warm tears I'll melt the snow
And keep eternal springtime on thy face,
So thou refuse to drink my dear sons' blood.

When daisies pied and violets blue

Song of Winter, *Love's Labour's Lost*

When icicles hang by the wall,
  And Dick the shepherd blows his nail,
And Tom bears logs into the hall,
  And milk comes frozen home in pail;
When blood is nipped, and ways be foul,
Then nightly sings the staring owl
  Tu-whit!
Tu-whit, tu-woo – a merry note,
While greasy Joan doth keel the pot

When all aloud the wind doth blow,
  And coughing drowns the parson's saw,
And birds sit brooding in the snow,
  And Marian's nose looks red and raw;
When roasted crabs hiss in the bowl,
Then nightly sings the staring owl
  Tu-whit!
Tu-whit, tu-woo – a merry note,
While greasy Joan doth keel the pot.

Chapter 5

GOATS AND MONKEYS

In Shakespeare's plays, animals often steal the show. In one, a clown enters with a real dog – called Crab. In another, a play rehearsal (featuring the difficult role of a lion) is disrupted by one of the actors entering with an ass's head. In a third, a character is chased off stage by a bear. But Shakespeare never forgot that a human being is just another "poor, bare, forked animal."

My kingdom for a horse!

King Richard, *Richard III*

A horse! A horse! My kingdom for a horse!

At one fell swoop

Macduff, *Macbeth*

What? All my pretty chickens and their dam
At one fell swoop?

A wilderness of tigers

Titus, *Titus Andronicus*

Why, foolish Lucius, dost not perceive
That Rome is but a wilderness of tigers?
Tigers must prey, and Rome affords no prey
But me and mine.

The bird of dawning singeth all night long

Horatio, *Hamlet*

It faded on the crowing of the cock.
Some say that ever 'gainst that season comes
Wherein our Saviour's birth is celebrated,
The bird of dawning singeth all night long.
And then, they say, no spirit dare stir abroad,
The nights are wholesome, then no planets strike,
No fairy takes, nor witch hath power to charm,
So hallowed and so gracious is the time.

The bird of night did sit even at noonday

Casca, *Julius Caesar*

Against the Capitol I met a lion
Who glazed upon me, and went surly by
Without annoying me. And there were drawn
Upon a heap a hundred ghastly women,
Transformed with their fear, who swore they saw
Men all in fire walk up and down the streets.
And yesterday the bird of night did sit
Even at noonday upon the market-place,
Hooting and shrieking.

The cat with eyne of burning coal

Gower the Chorus, *Pericles, Prince of Tyre*

The cat with eyne of burning coal
Now couches 'fore the mouse's hole,
And crickets at the oven's mouth
Sing the blither for their drouth.

Very like a whale

Polonius, *Hamlet*

HAMLET: Do you see yonder cloud that's almost in shape of a camel?
POLONIUS: By the mass, and 'tis like a camel indeed.
HAMLET: Methinks it is like a weasel.
POLONIUS: It is backed like a weasel.
HAMLET: Or like a whale?
POLONIUS: Very like a whale.

Not a mouse stirring

Francisco, *Hamlet*

BARNARDO: Have you had quiet guard?
FRANCISCO: Not a mouse stirring.

The poor cat i' th' adage

Lady Macbeth, *Macbeth*

Wouldst thou have that
Which thou esteem'st the ornament of life,
And live a coward in thine own esteem,
Letting "I dare not" wait upon "I would",
Like the poor cat i' th' adage.

The Mousetrap

Prince Hamlet, *Hamlet*

HAMLET: No, no, they do but jest, poison in jest, no offence in the world.
KING: What do you call the play?
HAMLET: The Mousetrap.

Be it on lion, bear, or wolf, or bull

Oberon, *A Midsummer Night's Dream*

Having once this juice,
I'll watch Titania when she is asleep,
And drop the liquor of it in her eyes.
The next thing then she waking looks upon –
Be it on lion, bear, or wolf, or bull,
On meddling monkey, or on busy ape –
She shall pursue it with the soul of love.

The toad, ugly and venomous

Duke, *As You Like It*

Sweet are the uses of adversity,
Which like the toad, ugly and venomous,
Wears yet a precious jewel in his head;
And this our life, exempt from public haunt,
Finds tongues in trees, books in the running brooks,
Sermons in stones, and good in everything.

Boys pursuing summer butterflies

Cominius, *Coriolanus*

He is their god. He leads them like a thing
Made by some other deity than nature,
That shapes man better; and they follow him
Against us brats, with no less confidence
Than boys pursuing summer butterflies,
Or butchers killing flies.

As flies to wanton boys are we to the gods

Gloucester, *King Lear*

As flies to wanton boys are we to the gods.
They kill us for their sport.

Eye of newt, and toe of frog

Witches' Spell, *Macbeth*

Double, double, toil and trouble
Fire, burn and cauldron bubble.
Fillet of a fenny snake,
In the cauldron boil and bake.
Eye of newt, and toe of frog,
Wool of bat, and tongue of dog,
Adder's fork and blind-worm's sting,
Lizard's leg and owlet's wing,
For a charm of powerful trouble,
Like a hell-broth boil and bubble.
Double, double, toil and trouble
Fire, burn and cauldron bubble.

Weaving spiders come not here

Fairies' Song, *A Midsummer Night's Dream*

You spotted snakes with double tongue,
Thorny hedge-hogs, be not seen;
Newts and blind-worms do no wrong,
Come not near our fairy queen!

Weaving spiders come not here,
Hence you long-legged spinners, hence!
Beetles black, approach not near
Worm nor snail do no offence.

Canst tell how an oyster makes his shell?

The Fool, *King Lear*

FOOL: Canst tell how an oyster makes his shell?
LEAR: No.
FOOL: Nor I neither; but I can tell why a snail has a house.
LEAR: Why?
FOOL: Why, to put's head in. Not to give it away to his daughters, and leave his horns without a case.

The world's mine oyster

Pistol, *The Merry Wives of Windsor*

Why then the world's mine oyster, which I with sword will open.

To be a dog, a mule, a cat

Thersites, *Troilus and Cressida*

To be a dog, a mule, a cat, a fitchew, a toad, a lizard, an owl, a puttock, or a herring without a roe, I would not care. But to be Menelaus, I would conspire against destiny! Ask me not what I should be, if I were not Thersites. For I care not to be the louse of a lazar, so I were not Menelaus.

I will wear my heart upon the sleeve

Iago, *Othello*

Were I the Moor, I would not be Iago.
In following him I follow but myself:
Heaven is my judge, not I for love and duty
But seeming so, for my peculiar end,
For when my outward action doth demonstrate
The native act and figure of my heart
In complement extern, 'tis not long after
But I will wear my heart upon the sleeve
For daws to peck at. I am not what I am.

Poor harmless fly

Titus, *Titus Andronicus*

TITUS: What dost thou strike at, Marcus, with thy knife?
MARCUS: At that I have killed, my lord: a fly.
TITUS: Out on thee, murderer! Thou kill'st my heart.
Mine eyes are cloyed with view of tyranny.
A deed of death done on the innocent
Becomes not Titus' brother. Get thee gone.
I see thou art not for my company.
MARCUS: Alas, my lord, I have but killed a fly.
TITUS: "But"?
How if that fly had a father and mother?
How would he hang his slender gilded wings
And buzz lamenting doings in the air?
Poor harmless fly,
That with his pretty buzzing melody
Came here to make us merry, and thou hast killed him.

We two alone will sing like birds i' th' cage

Lear, *King Lear*

Come let's away to prison;
We two alone will sing like birds i' th' cage.
When thou dost ask me blessing, I'll kneel down
And ask of thee forgiveness. So we'll live,
And pray, and sing, and tell old tales, and laugh
At gilded butterflies, and hear poor rogues
Talk of court news. And we'll talk with them too,
Who loses and who wins; who's in, who's out;
And take upon's the mystery of things,
As if we were God's spies. And we'll wear out,
In a walled prison, packs and sects of great ones
That ebb and flow by the moon.

Imitate the action of the tiger . . .

King Henry, *Henry V*

Once more unto the breach, dear friends, once more,
Or close the wall up with our English dead!
In peace there's nothing so becomes a man
As modest stillness and humility.
But when the blast of war blows in our ears,
Then imitate the action of the tiger.
Stiffen the sinews, conjure up the blood,
Disguise fair nature with a hard-favoured rage!

. . . Like greyhounds in the slips

King Henry, *Henry V*

And you, good yeomen,
Whose limbs were made in England, show us here
The mettle of your pasture. Let us swear
That you are worth your breeding – which I doubt not,
For there is none of you so mean and base
That hath not noble lustre in your eyes.
I see you stand like greyhounds in the slips,
Straining upon the start. The game's afoot.
Follow your spirit, and upon this charge
Cry, "God for Harry! England, and Saint George!"

A poor, bare, forked animal

Lear, *King Lear*

Thou wert better in a grave than to answer with thy uncovered body this extremity of the skies. Is man no more than this? Consider him well. Thou owest the worm no silk, the beast no hide, the sheep no wool, the cat no perfume. Ha! Here's three on's are sophisticated. Thou art the thing itself. Unaccommodated man is no more but such a poor, bare, forked animal as thou art!

The paragon of animals

Prince Hamlet, *Hamlet*

What a piece of work is man! How noble in reason, how infinite in faculty, in form and moving how express and admirable, in action how like an angel, in apprehension how like a god – the beauty of the world, the paragon of animals! And yet to me what is this quintessence of dust? Man delights not me – no, nor women neither, though by your smiling you seem to say so.

The wren goes to't

Lear, *King Lear*

The wren goes to't and the small gilded fly
Does lecher in my sight.
Let copulation thrive!

Well said, old mole

Prince Hamlet, *Hamlet*

GHOST [*under the stage*]: Swear!
HAMLET: Well said old mole! Canst work i' th' earth so fast?

A full-acorned boar

Posthumous, *Cymbeline*

I thought her
As chaste as unsunned snow. Oh, all the devils!
This yellow Iachimo, in an hour, was't not?
Or less, at first? Perchance he spoke not, but
Like a full-acorned boar, a German one,
Cried "Oh!" and mounted.

Like an angry ape

Isabella, *Measure for Measure*

Could great men thunder
As Jove himself does, Jove would ne'er be quiet,
For every pelting petty officer
Would use his heaven for thunder, nothing but
thunder.
Merciful Heaven,
Thou rather with thy sharp and sulphurous bolt
Splits the unwedgeable and gnarled oak,
Than the soft myrtle. But man, proud man,
Dressed in a little brief authority,
Most ignorant of what he's most assured
(His glassy essence) like an angry ape
Plays such fantastic tricks before high Heaven
As makes the angels weep; who, with our spleens,
Would all themselves laugh mortal.

The green-eyed monster

Iago, *Othello*

O, beware, my lord, of jealousy.
It is the green-eyed monster which doth mock
The meat it feeds on.

This pale faint swan

Prince Henry, *King John*

'Tis strange that death should sing.
I am the cygnet to this pale faint swan
Who chants a doleful hymn to his own death,
And from the organ-pipe of frailty sings
His soul and body to their lasting rest.

The swan's black legs

Aaron the Moor, *Titus Andronicus*

Coal-black is better than another hue
In that it scorns to bear another hue.
For all the water in the ocean
Can never turn the swan's black legs to white,
Although she lave them hourly in the flood.

That bottled spider

Queen Margaret, *Richard III*

Why strew'st thou sugar on that bottled spider,
Whose deadly web ensnareth thee about?
Fool, fool, thou whet'st a knife to kill thyself.
The day will come that thou shalt wish for me
To help thee curse this poisonous bunch-backed toad.

Let foolish gnats make sport

Antipholus of Syracuse, *The Comedy of Errors*

When the sun shines, let foolish gnats make sport,
But creep in crannies when he hides his beams.

Sparrows must not build in his house-eaves

Lucio, *Measure for Measure*

I would the Duke we talk of were returned. This ungenitured agent will unpeople the province with continency. Sparrows must not build in his house-eaves, because they are lecherous.

The temple-haunting martlet . . .

Banquo, *Macbeth*

DUNCAN: This castle hath a pleasant seat. The air
Nimbly and sweetly recommends itself
Unto our gentle senses.
BANQUO: This guest of summer,
The temple-haunting martlet, does approve
By his loved mansionry that the heavens' breath
Smells wooingly here. No jutty, frieze,
Buttress nor coign of vantage but this bird
Hath made his pendant bed and procreant cradle.
Where they most breed and haunt I have observed
The air is delicate.

. . . The raven himself is hoarse

Lady Macbeth, *Macbeth*

The raven himself is hoarse
That croaks the fatal entrance of Duncan
Under my battlements. Come, you spirits
That tend on mortal thoughts, unsex me here,
And fill me from the crown to the toe top-full
Of direst cruelty.

The croaking raven doth bellow for revenge

Prince Hamlet, *Hamlet*

Begin, murderer. Leave thy damnable faces and begin.
Come, the croaking raven doth bellow for revenge.

The sourest-natured dog that lives

Lance, *The Two Gentlemen of Verona*

Enter LANCE *with his dog* CRAB

LANCE: I think Crab, my dog, be the sourest-natured dog that lives. My mother weeping, my father wailing, my sister crying, our maid howling, our cat wringing her hands, and all our house in a great perplexity, yet did not this cruel-hearted cur shed one tear. He is a stone, a very pebble-stone, and has no more pity in him than a dog!

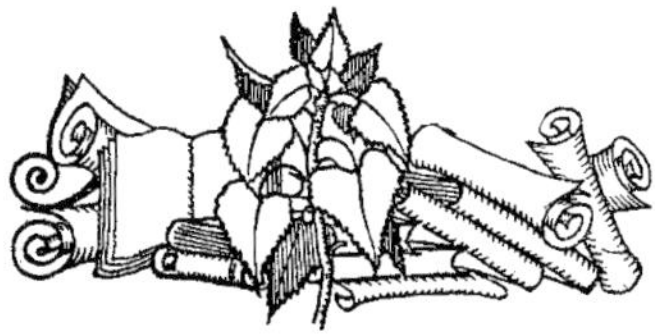

A dog's obeyed in office

Lear, *King Lear*

LEAR: Thou hast seen a farmer's dog bark at a beggar?
GLOUCESTER: Ay, sir.
LEAR: And the creature run from the cur?
There thou might'st behold
The great image of Authority:
A dog's obeyed in office.
Thou rascal beadle, hold thy bloody hand!
Why dost thou lash that whore? Strip thine own back;
Thou hotly lusts to use her in that kind
For which thou whipp'st her. The usurer hangs the
  cozener.
Thorough tattered clothes small vices do appear;
Robes and furred gowns hide all. Plate sin with gold
And the strong lance of justice hurtless breaks;
Arm it in rags, a pigmy's straw does pierce it.

The armed rhinoceros

Macbeth, seeing Banquo's Ghost, *Macbeth*

What man dare, I dare.
Approach thou like the rugged Russian bear,
The armed rhinoceros, or th' Hyrcan tiger;
Take any shape but that, and my firm nerves
Shall never tremble.

Like rats that ravin down their proper bane

Claudio, *Measure for Measure*

Liberty,
As surfeit, is the father of much fast.
So every scope by the immoderate use
Turns to restraint. Our natures do pursue,
Like rats that ravin down their proper bane,
A thirsty evil; and when we drink, we die.

How now? A rat?

Prince Hamlet, stabbing Polonius, *Hamlet*

How now? A rat? Dead for a ducat, dead!

There be land rats and water rats

Shylock, *The Merchant of Venice*

But ships are but boards, sailors but men. There be land rats and water rats, water thieves and land thieves – I mean pirates – and then there is the peril of waters, winds, and rocks. The man is, notwithstanding, sufficient. Three thousand ducats. I think I may take his bond.

Th' imperious seas breed monsters

Imogen, *Cymbeline*

These are kind creatures. Gods, what lies I have heard!
Our courtiers say all's savage but at court:
Experience, O thou disprov'st report!
Th' imperious seas breed monsters; for the dish
Poor tributary rivers as sweet fish.

~

So looks the pent-up lion

Rutland, *Henry VI, Part Three*

Rutland falls to the ground
CLIFFORD: How now? Is he dead already?
Or is it fear that makes him close his eyes?
RUTLAND: So looks the pent-up lion o'er the wretch
That trembles under his devouring paws,
And so he walks, insulting o'er his prey,
And so he comes to rend his limbs asunder.
Ah, gentle Clifford, kill me with thy sword
And not with such a threat'ning look.

The crow doth sing as sweetly as the lark

Portia, *The Merchant of Venice*

PORTIA: Music. Hark.
NERISSA: It is your music, madam, of the house.
PORTIA: Nothing is good, I see, without respect.
Methinks it sounds much sweeter than by day.
NERISSA: Silence bestows that virtue on it, madam.
PORTIA: The crow doth sing as sweetly as the lark
When neither is attended; and I think
The nightingale, if she should sing by day,
When every goose is cackling, would be thought
No better a musician than the wren.
How many things by season seasoned are
To their right praise and true perfection!

The crows and choughs that wing the midway air

Edgar, *King Lear*

How fearful
And dizzy 'tis to cast one's eyes so low!
The crows and choughs that wing the midway air
Show scarce so gross as beetles. Halfway down
Hangs one that gathers samphire, dreadful trade!
Methinks he seems no bigger than his head.
The fishermen that walk upon the beach
Appear like mice, and yond tall anchoring bark
Diminished to a cock, her cock a buoy
Almost too small for sight.

Two mighty eagles fell

Cassius, *Julius Caesar*

Coming from Sardis, on our former ensigns
Two mighty eagles fell, and there they perched,
Gorging and feeding from our soldiers' hands,
Who to Philippi here consorted us.
This morning are they fled away and gone,
And in their steads do ravens, crows and kites
Fly o'er our heads and downward look on us,
As we were sickly prey. Their shadows seem
A canopy most fatal, under which
Our army lies ready to give up the ghost.

A thing most strange and certain

Ross, Macbeth

OLD MAN: 'Tis unatural,
Even like the deed that's done. On Tuesday last
A falcon, tow'ring in her pride of place,
Was by a mousing owl hawked at and killed.
ROSS: And Duncan's horses (a thing most strange and certain)
Beauteous and swift, the minions of their race,
Turned wild in nature, broke their stalls, flung out,
Contending 'gainst obedience, as they would
Make war with mankind.
OLD MAN: 'Tis said they ate each other.
ROSS: They did so, to th'amazement of mine eyes
That looked upon't.

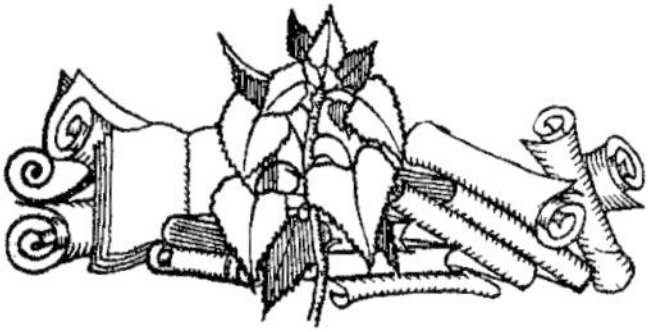

Let me play the lion too!

Bottom, *A Midsummer Night's Dream*

SNUG: Have you the lion's part written? Pray you, if it be, give it me; for I am slow of study.
QUINCE: You may do it extempore, for it is nothing but roaring.
BOTTOM: Let me play the lion too! I will roar that I will do any man's heart good to hear me. I will roar that I will make the Duke say, "Let him roar again, let him roar again."
QUINCE: An' you should do it too terribly you would fright the Duchess and the ladies that they would shriek, and that were enough to hang us all.
ALL: That would hang us, every mother's son.
BOTTOM: I grant you, friends, if you should fright the ladies out of their wits they would have no more discretion but to hang us, but I will aggravate my voice so that I will roar you as gently as any sucking dove. I will roar you an' twere any nightingale.

Baboon and monkey

Apemantus, *Timon of Athens*

Aches contract and starve your supple joints!
That there should be small love 'mongst these sweet
knaves,
And all this courtesy! The strain of man's bred out
Into baboon and monkey.

As prime as goats, as hot as monkeys

Iago, *Othello*

IAGO: Where's satisfaction?
It is impossible you should see this,
Were they as prime as goats, as hot as monkeys,
As salt as wolves in pride, and fools as gross
As ignorance made drunk. But, as I say,
If imputation, and strong circumstances
Which lead directly to the door of truth
Will give you satisfaction, you might ha't.
OTHELLO: Give me a living reason she's disloyal!

The engendering of toads

Ajax, *Troilus and Cressida*

AJAX: I do hate a proud man as I do hate the engendering of toads.
NESTOR: And yet he loves himself: is't not strange?

~

The chameleon's dish

Prince Hamlet, *Hamlet*

CLAUDIUS: How fares our cousin Hamlet?
HAMLET: Excellent, i'faith, of the chameleon's dish. I eat the air, promise-crammed. You cannot feed capons so.

~

I am as melancholy as a gib cat

Falstaff, *Henry IV, Part One*

FALSTAFF: Sblood! I am as melancholy as a gib cat, or a lugged bear.
PRINCE HAL: Or an old lion, or a lover's lute.
FALSTAFF: Yea, or the drone of a Lincolnshire bag-pipe.

As a weasel sucks eggs

Jaques, *As You Like It*

I can suck melancholy out of a song as a weasel sucks eggs. More, I prithee, more.

The country cocks do crow

The Chorus, *Henry V*

Now entertain conjecture of a time
When creeping murmur and the poring dark
Fills the wide vessel of the universe.
From camp to camp through the foul womb of night
The hum of either army stilly sounds,
That the fixed sentinels almost receive
The secret whispers of each other's watch.
Fire answers fire, and through their paly flames
Each battle sees the other's umbered face.
Steed threatens steed in high and boastful neighs,
Piercing the night's dull ear. And from the tents
The armourers, accomplishing the knights,
With busy hammers closing rivets up,
Give dreadful note of preparation.
The country cocks do crow, the clocks do toll,
And the third hour of drowsy morning name.

Like monsters of the deep

Albany, *King Lear*

Wisdom and goodness to the vile seem vile;
Filths savour but themselves. What have you done?
Tigers, not daughters, what have you performed?
A father, and a gracious aged man,
Whose reverence even the head-lugged bear would
  lick –
Most barbarous, most degenerate! Have you madded?
Could my good brother suffer you to do it?
A man, a prince, by him so benefited?
If that the heavens do not their visible spirits
Send quickly down to tame these vile offences,
It will come.
Humanity must perforce prey on itself,
Like monsters of the deep.

The great ones eat up the little ones

First Fisherman, *Pericles, Prince of Tyre*

THIRD FISHERMAN: Master, I marvel how the fishes live in the sea.

FIRST FISHERMAN: Why, as men do a' land: the great ones eat up the little ones. I can compare our rich misers to nothing so fitly as to a whale: he plays and tumbles, driving the poor fry before him, and at last devours them all at a mouthful. Such whales have I heard on 'i th' land, who never leave gaping till they swallowed the whole parish-church, steeple, bells, and all.

PERICLES: A pretty moral.

Where's my serpent of old Nile?

Cleopatra, *Antony and Cleopatra*

O Charmian!
Where think'st thou he is now? Stands he, or sits he?
Or does he walk? Or is he on his horse?
O happy horse to bear the weight of Antony!
Do bravely, horse, for wot'st thou whom thou mov'st,
The demi-Atlas of this earth, the arm
And burgonet of men. He's speaking now,
Or murmuring, "Where's my serpent of old Nile?"
For so he calls me.

Therefore think him as a serpent's egg

Brutus, *Julius Caesar*

And since the quarrel
Will bear no colour for the thing he is,
Fashion it thus: that what he is, augmented,
Would run to these and these extremities;
And therefore think him as a serpent's egg,
Which hatched, would as his kind grow mischievous,
And kill him in the shell.

For so work the honey-bees

Archbishop of Canterbury, *Henry V*

For so work the honey-bees,
Creatures that by a rule in nature teach
The act of order to a peopled kingdom.
They have a king and officers of sorts,
Where some like magistrates correct at home,
Others like merchants venture trade abroad,
Others like soldiers, armed in their stings,
Make boot upon the summer's velvet buds,
Which pillage they with merry match bring home
To the tent-royal of their emperor,
Who busied in his majesty surveys
The singing masons building roofs of gold,
The civil citizens lading up the honey,
The poor mechanic porters crowding in
Their heavy burdens at his narrow gate,
The sad-eyed justice with his surly hum,
Delivering o'er to executors pale
The lazy yawning drone.

Where the bee sucks, there suck I

Ariel's Song, *The Tempest*

Where the bee sucks, there suck I
In the cowslip's bell I lie;
There I couch when owls do cry.
On the bat's back I do fly
After summer merrily:
Merrily merrily shall I live now
Under the blossom that hangs on the bough.

Buzz, buzz

Prince Hamlet, *Hamlet*

HAMLET: I will prophesy he comes to tell me of the players. Mark it. – You say right, sir, for o' Monday morning, 'twas so indeed.
POLONIUS: My lord, I have news to tell you.
HAMLET: My lord, I have news to tell you. When Roscius was an actor in Rome –
POLONIUS: The actors are come hither, my lord.
HAMLET: Buzz, buzz

The poor beetle, that we tread upon

Isabella, *Measure for Measure*

Dar'st thou die?
The sense of death is most in apprehension,
And the poor beetle that we tread upon
In corporal sufferance finds a pang as great
As when a giant dies.

Why should a dog, a horse, a rat, have life?

Lear, *King Lear*

And my poor fool is hanged! No, no life!
Why should a dog, a horse, a rat, have life
And thou no breath at all? Thou'lt come no more,
Never, never, never, never, never!

The hot horse, hot as fire . . .

Pirithous, *The Two Noble Kinsmen*

As he thus went counting
The flinty pavement, dancing, as 'twere, to th' music
His own hooves made (for, as they say, from iron
Came music's origin), what envious flint,
Cold as old Saturn and like him possessed
With fire malevolent, darted a spark,
Or what fierce sulphur else, to this end made,
I comment not. The hot horse, hot as fire,
Took toy at this and fell to what disorder
His power could give his will; bounds; comes on end;
Forgets school-doing, being therein trained
And of kind manage; pig-like he whines
At the sharp rowel, which he frets at rather
Than any jot obeys; seeks all foul means
Of boist'rous and rough jad'ry to disseat
His lord, that kept it bravely.

. . . On end he stands!

Pirithous, *The Two Noble Kinsmen*

When naught served,
When neither curb would crack, girth break, nor
    diff'ring plunges
Disroot his rider whence he grew, but that
He kept him 'tween his legs, on his hind hooves –
On end he stands! –
That Arcite's legs, being higher than his head,
Seemed with strange art to hang. His victor's wreath
Even then fell off his head; and presently
Backward the jade comes o'er and his full poise
Becomes the rider's load.

A fly by an eagle

Enobarbus, *Antony and Cleopatra*

MAECENAS: Eight wild boars roasted whole at a breakfast and but twelve persons there – is this true?
ENOBARBUS: This was but as a fly by an eagle. We had much more monstrous matter of feast, which worthily deserved noting.

Like an eagle in a dove-cote

Caius Martius, *Coriolanus*

Cut me to pieces, Volsces, men and lads,
Stain all your edges on me. "Boy"? False hound!
If you have writ your annals true, 'tis there,
That like an eagle in a dove-cote, I
Fluttered your Volscians in Corioles.
Alone I did it. "Boy"!

There is special providence in the fall of a sparrow

Prince Hamlet, *Hamlet*

Not a whit. We defy augury. There is special providence in the fall of a sparrow. If it be now, 'tis not to come; if it be not to come, it will be now; if it be not now, yet it will come. The readiness is all. Since no man of aught he leaves, knows aught, what is't to leave betimes? Let be.

I, as Snug the joiner, am a lion fell

Snug, A Midsummer Night's Dream

SNUG [*as Lion*]: You, ladies, you whose gentle hearts do fear
The smallest monstrous mouse that creeps on floor,
May now perchance both quake and tremble here
When lion rough in wildest rage doth roar.
Then know that I, as Snug the joiner, am
A lion fell, nor else no lion's dam.
For if I should as Lion come in strife
Into this place, 'twere pity on my life.
THESEUS: A very gentle beast, and of a good conscience!
DEMETRIUS: The very best at a beast, my lord, that e'er I saw!
LYSANDER: This lion is a very fox for his valour!
THESEUS: True, and a goose for his discretion!

Bear-like I must fight the course

Macbeth, *Macbeth*

They have tied me to a stake. I cannot fly,
But bear-like I must fight the course. What's he
That was not born of woman? Such a one
Am I to fear, or none.

A vapour sometime, like a bear, or lion

Antony, *Antony and Cleopatra*

ANTONY: Sometime we see a cloud that's dragonish,
A vapour sometime, like a bear, or lion,
A tower'd citadel, a pendent rock,
A forked mountain, or blue promontory
With trees upon't, that nod unto the world,
And mock our eyes with air. Thou hast seen these signs,
They are black vesper's pageants.
EROS: Ay my lord.
ANTONY: That which is now a horse, even with a
thought
The rack dislimns and makes it indistinct
As water is in water.

Exit, pursued by a bear

Stage-Direction, *The Winter's Tale*

ANTIGONUS: I never saw
The heavens so dim by day. A savage clamour!
Well may I get aboard. This is the chase.
I am gone for ever!
Exit, pursued by a bear

Chapter 6

EXEUNT OMNES

Shakespeare knew full well that "Exeunt Omnes" (or "everyone leaves") is more than just a stage-direction in Latin. "All the world's a stage," and men and women – even bears – all "have their exits and their entrances." And thereby hangs a tale.

And thereby hangs a tale

Touchstone, *As You Like It*

'Tis but an hour ago since it was nine,
And after one hour more, 'twill be eleven.
And so from hour to hour, we ripe and ripe
And then from hour to hour, we rot and rot:
And thereby hangs a tale.

Ripeness is all

Edgar, *King Lear*

EDGAR: What? In ill thoughts again? Men must endure
Their going hence, even as their coming hither.
Ripeness is all. Come on.
GLOUCESTER: And that's true too.

A careless trifle

Malcolm, *Macbeth*

Nothing in his life
Became him like the leaving it. He died
As one that had been studied in his death,
To throw away the dearest thing he owed,
As 'twere a careless trifle.

Et tu, Brute?

Caesar, *Julius Caesar*

CINNA: O Caesar!
CAESAR: Hence! Wilt thou lift up Olympus?
DECIUS: Great Caesar!
CAESAR: Doth not Brutus bootless kneel?
CASCA: Speak hands for me!
They stab Caesar
CAESAR: Et tu, Brute? Then fall Caesar.

Imperious Caesar, dead and turned to clay

Prince Hamlet, *Hamlet*

Imperious Caesar, dead and turned to clay
Might stop a hole to keep the wind away.
O that that earth which kept the world in awe
Should patch a wall t'expel the winter's flaw!

~

The sweet war-man is dead and rotten

Armado, *Love's Labour's Lost*

The sweet war-man is dead and rotten. Sweet chucks, beat not the bones of the buried. When he breathed he was a man.

Out, damned spot

Lady Macbeth, *Macbeth*

GENTLEWOMAN: It is an acccustomed action with her, to seem thus washing her hands. I have known her continue in this a quarter of an hour.
LADY MACBETH: Yet here's a spot.
DOCTOR: Hark, she speaks. I will set down what comes from her to satisfy my remembrance the more strongly.
LADY MACBETH: Out, damned spot, out I say. One, two – why then 'tis time to do't. Hell is murky. Fie, my lord, fie, a soldier and afeared? What need we fear who knows it, when none can call our power to account? Yet who would have thought the old man to have had so much blood in him?

Could not all this flesh keep in a little life?

Prince Hal, *Henry IV, Part One*

He spieth Falstaff on the ground
What, old acquaintance! Could not all this flesh
Keep in a little life? Poor Jack, farewell.
I could have better spared a better man.
O, I should have a heavy miss of thee,
If I were much in love with vanity.
Death hath not struck so fat a deer today,
Though many dearer in this bloody fray.
Embowelled will I see thee by and by.
Till then, in blood by noble Percy lie.
Falstaff riseth up

A plague o' both your houses!

Mercutio, *Romeo and Juliet*

ROMEO: I thought all for the best.
MERCUTIO: Help me into some house, Benvolio,
Or I shall faint. A plague o' both your houses!
They have made worms' meat of me!
I have it, and soundly too. Your houses!

For worms, brave Percy

Prince Hal, *Henry IV, Part One*

HOTSPUR: O Harry, thou hast robbed me of my youth!
I better brook the loss of brittle life
Than those proud titles thou hast won of me;
They wound my thoughts worse than thy sword my flesh:
But thought's the slave of life, and life, time's fool,
And time, that takes survey of all the world,
Must have a stop. O, I could prophesy,
But that the earthy and cold hand of death
Lies on my tongue. No, Percy, thou art dust,
And food for –
HAL: For worms, brave Percy. Fare thee well, great heart.

I am more an antique Roman than a Dane

Horatio, *Hamlet*

HAMLET: You that look pale and tremble at this chance,
That are but mutes or audience to this act,
Had I but time – as this fell sergeant, Death,
Is strict in his arrest – O, I could tell you –
But let it be. Horatio, I am dead,
Thou liv'st. Report me and my cause aright
To the unsatisfied.
HORATIO: Never believe it.
I am more an antique Roman than a Dane.
Here's yet some liquor left.

This was the noblest Roman of them all

Mark Antony on Brutus, *Julius Caesar*

This was the noblest Roman of them all.
All the conspirators save only he
Did that they did in envy of great Caesar;
He only, in a general honest thought
And common good to all, made one of them.
His life was gentle, and the elements
So mixed in him, that Nature might stand up
And say to all the world, "This was a man."

He was a man, take him for all in all

Prince Hamlet, *Hamlet*

HAMLET: My father – methinks I see my father.
HORATIO: Oh where, my lord?
HAMLET: In my mind's eye, Horatio.
HORATIO: I saw him once. He was a goodly king.
HAMLET: He was a man, take him for all in all.
I shall not look upon his like again.

Full fathom five thy father lies

Ariel's Song, *The Tempest*

Full fathom five thy father lies,
  Of his bones are coral made
Those are pearls that were his eyes:
  Nothing of him that doth fade,
But doth suffer a sea-change
  Into something rich and strange.
Sea-nymphs hourly ring his knell.

O Lord, methought what pain it was to drown

Clarence, *Richard III*

O Lord, methought what pain it was to drown:
What dreadful noise of waters in my ears,
What sights of ugly death within my eyes!
Methought I saw a thousand fearful wrecks,
Ten thousand men that fishes gnawed upon,
Wedges of gold, great anchors, heaps of pearl,
Inestimable stones, unvalued jewels,
All scattered in the bottom of the sea.
Some lay in dead men's skulls, and in the holes
Where eyes did once inhabit, there were crept –
As 'twere in scorn of eyes – reflecting gems,
That wooed the slimy bottom of the deep,
And mocked the dead bones that lay scattered by.

In that Jerusalem shall Harry die

King Henry IV, *Henry IV, Part Two*

KING: Doth any name particular belong
Unto the lodging where I first did swoon?
WARWICK: 'Tis called Jersualem, my noble lord.
KING: Laud be to God! Even there my life must end.
It hath been prophesied to me many years
I should not die but in Jerusalem,
Which vainly I supposed the Holy Land;
But bear me to that chamber; there I'll lie,
In that Jerusalem shall Harry die.

Good night, ladies, good night, sweet ladies

Ophelia, *Hamlet*

I hope all will be well. We must be patient. But I cannot choose but weep to think they should lay him i' th' cold ground. My brother should know of it. And so I thank you for your good counsel. Come, my coach! Good night, ladies, good night, sweet ladies, good night, good night.

Parting is such sweet sorrow

Juliet, *Romeo and Juliet*

ROMEO: I would I were your bird.
JULIET: Sweet, so would I.
Yet I should kill thee with much cherishing.
Good night, good night. Parting is such sweet sorrow
That I shall say good night till it be morrow.

I would have broke my eye-strings

Imogen, *Cymbeline*

PISANIO: For so long
As he could make me with this eye or ear,
Distinguish him from others, he did keep
The deck, with glove or hat or handkerchief
Still waving, as the fits and stirs of's mind
Could best express how slow his soul sailed on,
How swift his ship.
IMOGEN: Thou shouldst have made him
As little as a crow, or less, ere left
To after-eye him.
PISANIO: Madam, so I did.
IMOGEN: I would have broke mine eye-strings, cracked
them, but
To look upon him till the diminution
Of space had pointed him sharp as a needle;
Nay followed him till he had melted from
The smallness of a gnat to air, and then
Have turned mine eye and wept.

A wheel of fire

Lear, *King Lear*

CORDELIA: How fares your majesty?
LEAR: You do me wrong to take me out o' th' grave.
Thou art a soul in bliss, but I am bound
Upon a wheel of fire, that mine own tears
Do scald like molten lead.

~

How ill white hairs become a fool and jester

Henry V, *Henry IV, Part Two*

FALSTAFF: My King! My Jove! I speak to thee, my heart!
KING: I know thee not, old man. Fall to thy prayers.
How ill white hairs become a fool and jester.
I have long dreamt of such a kind of man,
So surfeit-swelled, so old, and so profane,
But being awaked I do despise my dream.
Make less thy body hence, and more thy grace.
Less gormandizing. Know the grave doth gape
For thee thrice wider than for other men.

I'll go to bed at noon

The Fool, *King Lear*

LEAR: Make no noise, make no noise; draw the
curtains: so, so.
We'll go to supper i' th' morning.
FOOL: And I'll go to bed at noon.

Put out the light, and then put out the light

Othello, *Othello*

It is the cause, the cause, my soul.
Let me not name it to you, you chaste stars,
It is the cause. Yet I'll not shed her blood
Nor scar that whiter skin of hers than snow,
And smooth as monumental alabaster.
Yet she must die, else she'll betray more men.
Put out the light, and then put out the light.
If I quench thee, thou flaming minister,
I can again thy former light restore
Should I repent me. But once put out thy light,
Thou cunning'st pattern of excelling nature,
I know not where is that Promethean heat
That can thy light relume. When I have plucked the
    rose
I cannot give it vital growth again,
It needs must wither. I'll smell thee on the tree.
O balmy breath, that dost almost persuade
Justice to break her sword! Once more, once more:
Be thus when thou art dead and I will kill thee
And live thee after. Once more, and that's the last.

Like a bright exhalation in the evening

Cardinal Wolsey, *Henry VIII*

I have touched the highest point of all my greatness,
And from that full meridian of my glory
I haste now to my setting. I shall fall
Like a bright exhalation in the evening,
And no man see me more.

Here burns my candle out

Clifford, *Henry VI, Part Three*

Enter Clifford wounded, with an arrow in his neck
Here burns my candle out; ay, here it dies,
Which, whiles it lasted, gave Henry light.

We have heard the chimes at midnight

Falstaff, *Henry IV, Part Two*

SHALLOW: And is Jane Nightwork alive?
FALSTAFF: She lives, Master Shallow.
SHALLOW: She never could away from me.
FALSTAFF: Never, never. She would always say she could not abide Master Shallow.
SHALLOW: By the mass, I could anger her to th' heart. She was then a bona-roba. Doth she hold her own well?
FALSTAFF: Old, old, Master Shallow.
SHALLOW: Nay, she must be old; she cannot choose but be old; certain she's old – and had Robin Nightwork by old Nightwork before I came to Clement's Inn.
SILENCE: That's fifty-five year ago.
SHALLOW: Ha, cousin Silence? That thou hadst seen that that this old knight and I have seen! Ha, Sir John, said I well?
FALSTAFF: We have heard the chimes at midnight, Master Shallow.

Come away, come away death

Feste's Song, *Twelfth Night*

Come away, come away death,
  And in sad cypress let me be laid.
Fly away, fly away breath,
  I am slain by a fair cruel maid.
My shroud of white, stuck all with yew,
  O prepare it.
My part of death no one so true
  Did share it.

Not a flower, not a flower sweet
  On my black coffin let there be strewn.
Not a friend, not a friend greet
  My poor corpse, where my bones shall be thrown.
A thousand thousand sighs to save,
  Lay me, O where
Sad true lover never find my grace,
  To weep there.

Be absolute for death . . .

Duke, *Measure for Measure*

Be absolute for death. Either death or life
Shall thereby be the sweeter. Reason thus with life.
If I do lose thee, I do lose a thing
That none but fools would keep. A breath thou art,
Servile to all the skyey influences
That dost this habitation where thou keep'st
Hourly afflict. Merely, thou art death's fool,
For him thou labour'st by thy flight to shun,
And yet runn'st toward him still. Thou art not noble,
For all th' accommodations that thou bear'st
Are nursed by baseness. Thou'rt by no means valiant,
For thou dost fear the soft and tender fork
Of a poor worm. Thy best of rest is sleep
And that thou oft provok'st, yet grossly fear'st
Thy death, which is no more.

. . . Thou hast nor youth nor age

Duke, *Measure for Measure*

Thou hast nor youth nor age,
But as it were an after-dinner's sleep
Dreaming of both; for all thy blessed youth
Becomes as aged, and doth beg the alms
Of palsied eld; and when thou art old and rich,
Thou hast neither heat, affection, limb, nor beauty,
To make thy riches pleasant. What's yet in this
That bears the name of life? Yet in this life
Lie hid more thousand deaths; yet death we fear
That makes these odds all even.

The odds is gone

Cleopatra, *Antony and Cleopatra*

O, withered is the garland of the war,
The soldier's pole is fall'n. Young boys and girls
Are level now with men. The odds is gone,
And there is nothing left remarkable
Beneath the visiting moon.

The breaking of so great a thing

Caesar, *Antony and Cleopatra*

CAESAR: What is't thou say'st?
DECRETAS: I say, O Caesar, Antony is dead.
CAESAR: The breaking of so great a thing should make
A greater crack. The round world
Should have shook lions into civil streets,
And citizens to their dens. The death of Antony
Is not a single doom; in the name lay
A moiety of the world.

Farewell! Othello's occupation's gone

Othello, *Othello*

O now forever
Farewell the tranquil mind, farewell content,
Farewell the plumed troops and the big wars
That makes ambition virtue! O farewell,
Farewell the neighing steed and the shrill trump,
The spirit-stirring drum, th' ear-piercing fife,
The royal banner, and all quality,
Pride, pomp and circumstances of glorious war,
And O you mortal engines whose rude throats
Th' immortal Jove's clamours counterfeit
Farewell! Othello's occupation's gone.

Farewell! Thou art too dear for my possessing

Sonnet 87

Farewell! Thou art too dear for my possessing,
And like enough thou know'st thy estimate.
The charter of thy worth gives thee releasing,
My bonds in thee are too determinate.
For how do I hold thee but by thy granting,
And for that riches where is my deserving?
The cause of this fair gift in me is wanting,
And so my patent back again is swerving.
Thyself thou gav'st, thy own worth then not knowing,
Or me to whom thou gav'st it, else mistaking;
So thy great gift upon misprision growing
Comes home again, on better judgement making.
 Thus have I had thee as a dream doth flatter:
 In sleep a king, and waking no such matter.

The bloody dog is dead

Richmond, *Richard III*

God and our arms be praised, victorious friends!
The day is ours. The bloody dog is dead.

For never was a story of more woe

Prince of Verona, *Romeo and Juliet*

A glooming peace this morning with it brings.
The sun for sorrow will not show his head.
Go hence to have more talk of these sad things.
Some shall be pardoned, and some punished,
For never was a story of more woe
Than this of Juliet and her Romeo.
Exeunt Omnes

I bleed, sir, but not killed

Iago, *Othello*

LODOVICO: Where is this rash and most unfortunate man?
OTHELLO: That's he that was Othello. Here I am.
LODOVICO: Where is that viper? Bring the villain forth.
OTHELLO: I look down towards his feet, but that's fable.
If that thou beest a devil I cannot kill thee.
He wounds Iago
LODOVICO: Wrench his sword from him!
IAGO: I bleed, sir, but not killed.

He babbled of green fields

Hostess, *Henry V*

Nay sure, he's not in hell: he's in Arthur's bosom, if ever man went to Arthur's bosom. He made a finer end, and went away, an' it had been any christom child. He parted even just between twelve and one, even at the turning o' th' tide. For after I saw him fumble with the sheets and play with flowers and smile upon his fingers' end, I knew there was but one way. For his nose was as sharp as a pen, and he babbled of green fields.

"How now, Sir John?", quoth I, "what, man! Be o' good cheer." So he cried out, "God, God, God," three or four times. Now I (to comfort him) bid him he should not think of God, I hoped there was no need to trouble himself with any such thoughts yet. So he bade me lay more clothes on his feet: I put my hand into the bed and felt them, and they were as cold as any stone; then I felt to his knees, and so upward and upward and all was as cold as any stone.

Sad stories of the death of kings

King Richard, *Richard II*

For God's sake, let us sit upon the ground
And tell sad stories of the death of kings.
How some have been deposed, some slain in war,
Some haunted by the ghosts they have deposed,
Some poisoned by their wives, some sleeping killed,
All murdered. For within the hollow crown
That rounds the mortal temples of a king
Keeps Death his court. And there the antic sits,
Scoffing his state and grinning at his pomp,
Allowing him a breath, a little scene
To monarchize, be feared, and kill with looks,
Infusing him with self and vain conceit,
As if this flesh which walls about our life
Were brass impregnable; and humoured thus
Comes at the last, and with a little pin
Bores through his castle wall, and farewell, king.

To be or not to be, that is the question . . .

Prince Hamlet, *Hamlet*

To be or not to be, that is the question:
Whether 'tis nobler in the mind to suffer
The slings and arrows of outrageous fortune,
Or to take arms against a sea of troubles
And by opposing end them. To die – to sleep,
No more; and by a sleep to say we end
The heart-ache and the thousand natural shocks
That flesh is heir to. 'Tis a consummation
Devoutly to be wished. To die, to sleep;
To sleep, perchance to dream – ay there's the rub.
For in that sleep of death what dreams may come
When we have shuffled off this mortal coil
Must give us pause. There's the respect
That makes calamity of so long life.

. . . The undiscovered country

Prince Hamlet, *Hamlet*

For who would bear the whips and scorns of time,
Th' oppressor's wrong, the proud man's contumely,
The pangs of disprized love, the law's delay,
The insolence of office, and the spurns
That patient merit of th' unworthy takes,
When he himself might his quietus make
With a bare bodkin? Who would fardels bear,
To grunt and sweat under a weary life,
But that the dread of something after death,
The undiscovered country from whose bourn
No traveller returns, puzzles the will,
And makes us rather bear those ills we have
Than fly to others that we know not of?
Thus conscience doth make cowards of us all,
And thus the native hue of resolution
Is sicklied over with the pale cast of thought,
And enterprises of great pith and moment
With this regard their currents turn awry
And lose the name of action.

One that loved not wisely but too well

Othello, *Othello*

Soft you, a word or two before you go.
I have done the state some service, and they know't.
No more of that. I pray you, in your letters,
When you shall these unlucky deeds relate,
Speak of me as I am. Nothing extenuate,
Nor set down aught in malice. Then must you speak
Of one that loved not wisely but too well,
Of one not easily jealous but, being wrought,
Perplexed in the extreme; of one whose hand,
Like the base Judean, threw a pearl away
Richer than all his tribe; of one whose subdued eyes,
Albeit used to the melting mood,
Drops tears as fast as the Arabian trees
Their med'cinable gum. Set you down this,
And say besides that in Aleppo once
Where a malignant and a turbaned Turk
Beat a Venetian and traduced the state,
I took by th' throat the circumcised dog
And smote him, thus – *He stabs himself*

The wheel is come full circle

Edmund, *King Lear*

EDGAR: The Gods are just, and of our pleasant vices
Make instruments to plague us;
The dark and vicious place where thee he got
Cost him his eyes.
EDMUND: Th'ast spoken right, 'tis true.
The wheel is come full circle.

Lay on, Macduff

Macbeth, *Macbeth*

MACDUFF: Then yield thee, coward,
And live to be the show and gaze o' th' time.
We'll have thee as our rarer monsters are,
Painted upon a pole, and underwrit
"Here may you see the tyrant".
MACBETH: I will not yield
To kiss the ground before young Malcolm's feet,
And to be baited with the rabble's curse.
Though Birnam Wood be come to Dunsinane,
And thou opposed being of no woman born,
Yet will I try the last. Before my body
I throw my warlike shield. Lay on, Macduff,
And damned be him that first cries, "Hold, enough!"

The whirligig of time

Feste, *Twelfth Night*

FESTE: And thus the whirligig of time brings in his revenges.
MALVOLIO: I'll be revenged on the whole pack of you!

Flights of angels sing thee to thy rest

Horatio, *Hamlet*

HAMLET: The rest is silence.
HORATIO: Now cracks a noble heart. Good night, sweet prince,
And flights of angels sing thee to thy rest.

Who is't can say "I am at the worst"?

Edgar, *King Lear*

OLD MAN: How now? Who's there?
EDGAR: O gods! Who is't can say "I am at the worst"?
I am worse than e'er I was.
OLD MAN: 'Tis poor mad Tom.
EDGAR: And worse I may be yet. The worse is not
So long as we can say "This is the worst."

The rack of this tough world

Kent, *King Lear*

LEAR: Do you see this? Look on her. Look, her lips!
Look there, look there! *He dies*
EDGAR: He faints. My lord! My lord!
KENT: Vex not his ghost. O, let him pass. He hates him
That would upon the rack of this tough world
Stretch him out longer.

A lass unparalleled

Charmian, *Antony and Cleopatra*

CLEOPATRA: Peace, peace!
Dost thou not see my baby at my breast,
That sucks the nurse asleep?
CHARMIAN: O, break, break!
CLEOPATRA: As sweet as balm, as soft as air, as gentle.
O Antony! nay I will take thee too.
She puts another asp to her breast
What, should I stay – *She dies*
CHARMIAN: In this vile world? So fare thee well.
Now boast thee, death, in thy possession lies
A lass unparalleled. Downy windows, close,
And golden Phoebus never be beheld
Of eyes again so royal. Your crown's awry.
I'll mend it and then play.

The sad dirge of her certain ending

The Rape of Lucrece

And now this pale swan in her wat'ry nest
Begins the sad dirge of her certain ending.

But this rough magic I here abjure

Prospero, *The Tempest*

Graves at my command
Have waked their sleepers, oped, and let 'em forth
By my so potent art. But this rough magic
I here abjure. And when I have required
Some heavenly music – which even now I do –
To work mine end upon their senses that
This airy charm is for, I'll break my staff,
Bury it certain fathoms in the earth,
And deeper than did ever plummet sound
I'll drown my book.

If we shadows have offended

Puck, *A Midsummer Night's Dream*

If we shadows have offended,
Think but this, and all is mended.
That you have but slumbered here
While these visions did appear.
And this weak and idle theme,
No more yielding but a dream.
Gentles, do not reprehend,
If you pardon, we will mend.
And, as I am an honest Puck,
If we have unearned luck
Now to 'scape the serpent's tongue,
We will make amends ere long;
Else the Puck a liar call.
So goodnight unto you all.

No longer mourn for me when I am dead

Sonnet 71

No longer mourn for me when I am dead
Than you shall hear the surly sullen bell
Give warning to the world that I am fled
From this vile world, with vilest worms to dwell.
Nay, if you read this line, remember not
The hand that writ it. For I love you so
That I in your sweet thoughts would be forgot
If thinking on me then should make you woe.
O if I say, you look upon this verse
When I perhaps compounded am with clay,
Do not so much as my poor name rehearse,
But let your love even with my life decay,
  Lest the wise world should look into your moan
  And mock you with me after I am gone.

Pass by and curse thy fill, but pass

Timon's epitaph, *Timon of Athens*

Here lies a wretched corpse,
  Of wretched soul bereft.
Seek not my name. A plague consume
  You wicked caitiffs left!
Here lie I, Timon, who alive
  All living men did hate.
Pass by and curse thy fill, but pass
  And stay not here thy gait.

And curst be he who moves these bones

Shakespeare's tomb, Stratford-upon-Avon

Good friend, for Jesus sake forbear
To dig the dust enclosed here.
Blest be the man who spares these stones,
And curst be he who moves these bones.

Which of you have done this?

Macbeth, *Macbeth*

The Ghost of Banquo enters, and sits in Macbeth's place

LENNOX: What is't that moves your highness?
MACBETH: Which of you have done this?
LORDS: What, my good lord?
MACBETH: Thou canst not say I did it. Never shake
Thy gory locks at me.

Ay, at Philippi

Caesar's Ghost, *Julius Caesar*

Enter the Ghost of Caesar

BRUTUS: How ill this taper burns. Ha! Who comes here?
I think it is the weakness of mine eyes
That shapes this monstrous apparition.
It comes upon me. Art thou anything?
Art thou some god, some angel, or some devil,
That mak'st my blood cold, and my hair to stare?
Speak to me what thou art.
GHOST: Thy evil spirit, Brutus.
BRUTUS: Why com'st thou?
GHOST: To tell thee thou shalt see me at Philippi.
BRUTUS: Well – then I shall see thee again?
GHOST: Ay, at Philippi.

Dream on

Buckingham's Ghost, *Richard III*

Enter the Ghost of Buckingham to King Richard
GHOST: The first was I that helped thee to the crown,
The last was I that felt thy tyranny.
Oh, in the battle think of Buckingham,
And die in terror of thy guiltiness.
Dream on, dream on of bloody deeds and death;
Fainting, despair; despairing, yield thy breath.
Richard starteth up out of a dream
RICHARD: Give me another horse! Bind up my wounds!
Have, mercy, Jesu! – Soft, I did but dream.
O coward conscience, how dost thou afflict me!
The light's but blue. It is now dead midnight.
Cold fearful drops stand on my trembling flesh.
What do I fear? Myself? There's none else by.
Richard loves Richard, that is, I and I.
Is there a murderer here? No. Yes – I am!
Then fly! What? From myself?

My father in his habit as he lived

Prince Hamlet, *Hamlet*

GERTRUDE: To whom do you speak this?
HAMLET: Do you see nothing there?
GERTRUDE: Nothing at all, yet all I that is I see.
HAMLET: Nor did you nothing hear?
GERTRUDE: No, nothing but ourselves.
HAMLET: Why, look you there! Look how it steals away.
My father in his habit as he lived!
Look where it goes even now out at the portal.
Exit Ghost
GERTRUDE: This is the very coinage of your brain!

The name and not the thing

Helena, *All's Well That Ends Well*

KING: Is there no exorcist
Beguiles the truer office of mine eyes?
HELENA: No, my good lord.
'Tis but the shadow of a wife you see.
The name and not the thing.

Is this the final end?

Kent, *King Lear*

KENT: Is this the final end?
EDGAR: Or image of that horror?
ALBANY: Fall and cease.